MW00629297

TAKING THE FEAR OUT OF THE NIGHT

Understanding and Coping with Nightmares

by

Renate Daniel

Taking the Fear Out of the Night

Understanding and Coping with Nightmares

by

Renate Daniel

DAIMON
Verlag

Title of the German language original:
Der Nacht den Schrecken nehmen. Albträume verstehen und bewältigen
© 2013 Schwabenverlag AG, Patmos Verlag, Ostfildern.

English translation by Mary Dobrian.

Daimon Verlag and the author are grateful to the Stiftung zur Förderung der Psychologie von C.G. Jung as well as a donor wishing to remain unnamed for their financial support.
For permission to use the cover image, "At the Door" by Peter Birkhäuser, we thank Eva Wertenschlag.

Cover illustration: "At the Door"
© Stiftung Peter und Sybille Birkhäuser-Oeri, www.birkhäuser-oeri.ch, from *Windows on Eternity, The Paintings of Peter Birkhäuser,* by Eva Wertenschlag-Birkhäuser, Plate 25, page 109, Daimon, Einsiedeln 2009.

Photograph of the author © Michael Seitter.

First edition

Copyright © 2016 Daimon Verlag, Einsiedeln

ISBN 978-3-85630-760-8

For Michael

Contents

Introduction: Nightmares Demand a Response
– Three different examples

Nightmares are not unusual experiences: nearly one out of twenty people in Germany is plagued by nightmares on a regular basis. Not only adults, but children and adolescents as well, are affected by them.

If you are one of those affected: how do you feel when you awake from a nightmare – drenched in sweat, your heart racing, in a panic or with the feeling of a lead weight pressing on your chest? Do you try to forget the terrifying dream images as quickly as possible? Or, unable to escape the images of your nightmares, do you try to decipher their messages? How does a nightmare influence your behavior and your everyday life?

Nightmares can unsettle us – not only during the night, but also on the following day, leaving us feeling depressed, irritable or stressed. Understandably, we would prefer not to experience nightmares at all – and if they do occur, we want to shake them off as quickly as possible.

Yet how can we manage to be less troubled by nightmares? How should we deal with them?

If we view a nightmare as a disturbing, frightening or disconcerting question, our aim would be to find a satisfactory answer. Seen from this point of view, the wide variation of nightmares would correspond to a broad spectrum of questions and lead to a multitude of answers.

Small children often ask quite blunt questions: "Mommy is that man over there the devil?", "Why are you so fat?" or "Why doesn't the moon fall out of the sky?" Astonished children present adults with astonishing questions. They are curious, unbiased, and they pay no heed to conventions – just like our dreams. Once children enter school, the situation is reversed, and adults direct more questions at children in order to test their knowledge and abilities. While good pupils are more able to take this in stride, others fervently hope to be spared from their teachers' questions. And even young schoolchildren begin to notice that questions cannot only be stimulating, but they may also be unpleasantly penetrating. Such questions seem to bombard them like missiles: they cause pain, injury or shame.

In a similar manner, nightmares can ruthlessly invade our consciousness and cause us to tremble or become speechless or petrified. However, once the initial shock is past, it is often possible to ask ourselves or our nightmares: "Why am I dreaming such terrible things? What does this have to do with my life and my relationships?" If we scrutinize the destructive force in the most interested and unprejudiced manner possible, we will seldom remain powerless; rather, we will discover answers. And experience has shown that a person who finds a coherent answer to her nightmares will be able to sleep better again.

Upon receiving his award, the Hungarian director Bence Fliegauf – winner of the Silver Bear at the 2012 Berlin Film Festival – spoke incidentally about his own way of dealing with nightmares: "Whenever I wake up from a nightmare, I know that I need to make a film." Bence Fliegauf has found his own personal response to his nightmares: for him, it is important to examine a subject – perhaps the focal point of his dream – using an artistic approach and thereby create a film. His nightmares seem to present him with a work order: in a way, they are his own very personal method of job creation, to which he devotes himself with earnest commitment and zeal.

In the late 1990s, Olympic high bar champion Andreas Wecker responded to his nightmares in a completely different way. He repeatedly woke up bathed in sweat, remembering nightmare images of himself sitting crippled in a wheelchair. After subsequently sustaining severe bruises and hematomas during a practice session on the high bar, he did not hesitate long in deciding to end his athletic career. His decision was met with some incomprehension on the part of his trainers and colleagues. Andreas Wecker responded to his nightmares with an existential choice which radically altered his future.[1] Were Andreas Wecker's decision and reaction the correct ones? – especially given the fact that no one will ever know whether a serious accident might have occurred if he had remained active as a professional athlete?

As soon as a series of nightmares comes to an end – that is, as soon as the dreamer's soul has become calm – then he or she has generally found the "right answer." For those of us on the outside, this is not always understandable, since we are not able to experience the impressive power and intensity of the menacing nightmare images. Each of us dreams for himself alone, and we can only tell other people about our dream experiences – but we cannot take them with us into our dream worlds in order to convince them of our images' dramatic relevance first hand. Anyone who makes far-reaching decisions based on his or her nightmares is ultimately forced to fall back on his own subjective interpretation of the nightmare images. If he relies on his intuitive, instinctive feelings, or trusts in the collected knowledge of dreams and their interpretation which human beings have gathered for thousands of years, he will have useful tools for dealing constructively with his own nightmare images.

The psychiatrist Wanda Póltawska describes an alternative response to nightmares. Her nightmares always appeared at times when she was overworked and extremely exhausted. As soon as she allowed herself more time to rest, her nightmares disappeared again. However, many years earlier, she had a very different experience with her nightmares, which first occurred on the night of May 8, 1945. On that day, she had returned home from the Ravensbrück concentration camp and immediately began dreaming about her horrendous experiences in the camp. Because of these unbearable nightmares, she became increasingly afraid of going to sleep. In desperation, she took pencil and paper in hand. In the summer of 1945, after she had written down all of her terrible memories from her life in the camp, her nightmares promptly ceased.

Wanda Półtawska was once again able to sleep undisturbed, and in later years, her nightmares returned only at times when she had demanded too much of herself.[2]

Three people found individual responses to their nightmares which worked for each of them personally. They experienced the way in which horrific nocturnal images impose themselves unbidden on the sleeper, but also the way in which they disappear again as soon as their message has been deciphered.

1. What are Dreams?

The Waking, Sleeping and Dreaming Worlds

"You cannot build a dream; a dream builds itself."[3] With this statement, Friedrich Weinreb points to a central characteristic of dreams: dreams are, in fact, beyond our control. Regardless of whether we value them or prefer to be spared from them – control over whether or not they come is not in our hands. They appear whenever they wish and say whatever they want to.

Waking and Sleeping Worlds

Qualitatively, waking and sleeping are completely different worlds in terms of the experience of our ego. In a waking state, our ego has access to a reflexive consciousness and has various areas of action and decision-making at its disposal. This allows us to shape our lives deliberately and more or less actively. However, our free will breaks down at the very threshold of sleep. A person who is determined to fall asleep in order to be especially well rested on the following day will frequently lie awake for a long time. It is not uncommon for someone who is desperately trying to fall asleep to toss and turn tensely and restlessly from one side to the other.

We can only go to sleep when we let go, when we allow our ego to plunge into the unknown. This requires the ego to relinquish control. People who, for whatever reason, are always afraid of losing control over their lives, often have difficulty falling asleep. This fear of losing control is fundamentally plausible, since when we are asleep we are unprotected and at the mercy of others. Danger lurks first and foremost in the outside world. We can see this clearly in the case of wild animals that sleep out in the open. Without enemies, it would be possible, in principle, to sleep anywhere at any time without care. In nature, however, only a few animals have this luxury. Most animals do have enemies and therefore they either require a safe place to sleep, or they must be capable of waking rapidly in order to defend themselves or to flee. As long as this is guaranteed, a species can survive. In the early history of humankind, human beings were certainly in a similar situation. Nature was threatening, particularly when one was asleep. As soon as we are asleep, we can no longer perceive our environment through our senses. We do not hear or see if a person or an animal is approaching us with hostile intentions. If dangerous fumes are poisoning the air we breathe, we cannot smell them. We may not even necessarily be aware of dangerously cold temperatures. This is why, even today, homeless people can freeze to death on icy cold nights. In our sleep, we are not adequately protected from low temperatures. Human beings would probably have become extinct long ago had they not been able to take specific protective measures during the sleep state. Some historians assume that for large groups of human beings, a long, deep sleep only became possible once communities had been sufficiently secured by city walls and night watchmen.

Even today, we require a secure location of this kind in order to sleep without fear of assault. Rarely are we consciously aware of the fact that our bedrooms are a safe place that a stranger will generally not enter without invitation. However, anyone who has ever been surprised from his or her sleep by an intruder knows how long it can take to regain the necessary sense of security without which one could not think of sleeping. Following a nighttime attack, some people even need to move to a new home, because the intruder has completely destroyed their sense of security within their own four walls. Such experiences are an indication of how difficult it is to go to sleep in war zones or in places that have been exposed to natural disasters. People's faith in an undisturbed night's rest is completely lost, and it is very difficult to believe that one will wake up again unharmed.

However, a sleeping person is not only subjected to external threats. The lullaby, *"Guten Abend, gute Nacht"* ("Good evening, good night"), composed by Johannes Brahms in the nineteenth century reminds people in its original refrain, *"Morgen früh, wenn Gott will, wirst du wieder geweckt"* ("Tomorrow morning, God willing, you will awake again"), that whether or not they will wake up again is not under their control. Religious people and atheists alike know that the fundamental message of this refrain is true: it is possible to die in one's sleep, either by suffering a heart attack or because one's organs fail for some other reason. During sleep, one can drift away into death. In Antiquity, sleep (*Hypnos*) and gentle death (*Thanatos*) were considered to be brothers, and this old lullaby draws on that fundamental closeness between sleep and death – on their fateful connection. Nevertheless, it does not forget to wish the child a blissful sleep and sweet dreams.

Pleasant dreams are a good starting point for a peaceful and restorative sleep. Nightmares, on the other hand, can seriously disturb our sleep. Their images threaten us from within. Living intruders who enter our homes during the night are not the only beings who can send us into a panic; predatory figures from our dreams can do so as well. The immediate physical and psychological reactions to such dangers are very similar, whether they take place in reality or in a dream.

A person who is awakened by images of intruders frequently feels helpless and unprotected. These feelings are very real, despite the fact that when we awake, we quickly recognize that the criminals who threatened us were simply a product of our dreams. Sometimes, such dream intruders even prompt us to take action: we check to see whether our windows and doors are securely locked, in order to be sure that no one actually can enter our homes uninvited. The mere assurance that we have simply had a dream and that the burglars have invaded nothing more than our minds is not always sufficient to comfort us.

Consciousness, Unconsciousness and the Unconscious

We refer to our experiences during sleep as dreams. However, this definition is insufficient and imprecise, since we are familiar with a similar phenomenon during the waking state: the daydream. Dreaming, therefore, is not limited to sleep. We speak of "dreamers" when referring to those people who tend to immerse themselves in their fantasies during the day and allow themselves to be swept away by inner images rather than turning their attention to the external reality. Daydreaming is not always seen in a positive light. Parents and teachers in particular react with concern when a pupil concentrates too little on his or her lesson requirements because his fantasy world distracts him from these demands and tempts him to dawdle. What do these daydreams have in common with nighttime dreams, and what distinguishes the two from each another?

We can come closer to an answer when we take a closer look at the difference between consciousness and unconsciousness. If you concentrate on the words you are reading now, you will only be able to do so because you are awake and conscious. Therefore, consciousness and the waking state go hand in hand. Since waking is an essential prerequisite for consciousness in the sense that we refer to it here, we also speak of "waking consciousness." Metaphorically speaking, we can compare consciousness with the light from a lamp. In a waking state, our ego has, so to speak, a lamp in its hand, and can direct that light intentionally toward a certain object. This may be the world around us, but it may also be our body or our spiritual life. Everything that the lamplight makes visible is conscious. Thus, consciousness has to do with seeing clearly and being able to recognize things. Thanks to consciousness, we know that we exist. Furthermore, we know who we are, where we are, and we can recall the date and time of day. Consciousness gives us the ability to orient ourselves in time and space. Consciousness also provides us with other complex abilities: we are able to concentrate or be attentive, to think logically, assess situations and act deliberately, to name just a few.

Nevertheless, the lamp of consciousness only has a limited range, and therefore, by necessity, certain areas remain in darkness. In depth psychology, we refer to this entire dark area as the unconscious. We can illuminate some of these dark areas relatively easily with the help of our lamp. For example, when we try to remember something, we actively direct the light of our lamp toward our memory reservoir, which lies within the unconscious. As soon as we are able, for example, to remember a name, we have drawn this information into the light of consciousness. Our ability to remember proves that experiences or facts of which we were conscious in the past can sink into the unconscious and remain stored there. We have the ability to actively retrieve and recall a great deal of this information; other things remain in darkness, and we can no longer recall them explicitly even when we make a great effort to remember them.

The conscious process of remembering is characterized by explicit memories. Yet even when we can no longer explicitly recall an experience – that is, we can no longer make ourselves conscious of it – it has not disappeared or been erased. It remains preserved and is effective via our so-called "implicit memory." The difference between explicit and implicit memory can be seen especially clearly in people who have lost their capacity for explicit memory and can only remember things implicitly. For example, in 1911, the French neurologist Édouard Claparède reported on a brain-damaged patient who immediately forgot everything that she had just experienced. Every time he met with her, he had to introduce himself to her again, since she could no longer remember who he was. She was no longer capable of explicit memory. One day, he concealed a thumbtack in his hand while greeting her; naturally, the patient withdrew her hand in shock. On the following visit, she refused to give the doctor her hand. However, she was unable to explain her reason for doing so.[4]

14

Similarly, neuroscientist and Nobel laureate Roger Sperry was able to establish a difference between explicit and implicit memory in so-called "split-brain" patients.[5] In these patients, the group of nerve fibers[6] which connects the left and right hemispheres of the brain has been severed, with the result that the cognitive-linguistic abilities of the left hemisphere can no longer be connected to the emotional, pictorial impressions produced in the right hemisphere.

Roger Sperry showed pornographic pictures to a woman in whom the connection between the left and right brain hemispheres had been severed as the result of an operation. She turned red and began to giggle; yet she was not able to explain the reason why she reacted in this way. This example makes it clear that becoming conscious and remembering is a multi-step process: at the first level, we require healthy eyesight, intact brain regions and nerve channels[7] simply in order to perceive an image. If there is any defect in these areas of the body, we are blind. At the second level, we are able to comprehend the meaning of the image unconsciously and react to it appropriately.

Roger Sperry's patient must have "recognized" the pornographic image, since she reacted to it in a way that made sense. Likewise, Édouard Claparède's brain-damaged patient must have "recognized" the relationship between hand and pain; otherwise, she would not have refused the handshake. Both women "knew" something, but since they were not able to reach the third level, they did not know it explicitly. Only then would they have been capable of expressing their perceptions, experiences and memories in words and reflecting on the contexts and connections.

This reflexive or explicit consciousness in a waking state is what I am referring to when I use the image of lamplight. According to neuroscientific findings, reflexive consciousness appears to account for merely five percent of our mental activity and behavior. Even completely healthy people live predominately at an unconscious level, and most of the information with which we are bombarded is processed in the unconscious portion of our psyche and stored in our memory.[8] From there, information can find its way into our dreams, even if we were only implicitly conscious of it. However, dream experiences also wander back into our memories. It even seems that while we are dreaming, we consolidate our memories – that is, we can anchor abilities and practiced skills better in this way. Dreaming supports the learning process.[9]

Yet the unconscious which can reveal itself in our dreams does not only consist of forgotten or repressed personal experiences. It also contains dark regions into which the lamplight of our consciousness has never penetrated. This region includes everything which we do not yet know or consider possible. As soon as we have an idea or a flash of inspiration, something unconscious somehow enters the area that is illuminated by the lamp of our consciousness.

Creative people are very familiar with this phenomenon, and they wait in a state of free-floating attentiveness for the decisive moment when something interesting appears at the periphery of the beam of light. As soon as a person can see something universally significant emerging from the unconscious, he or she has the makings of a genius. This phenomenon is described in Daniel Kehlmann's novel *Measuring the World* (German: *Die Vermessung der Welt)*. When one of the novel's two protagonists, mathematician Carl Friedrich Gauß, suddenly achieves a stroke of mathematical insight during his wedding night, his wife experiences something unbelievable: she must watch as Gauß leaves the bed in order to write down the new mathematical formula. Even though he is ashamed of his behavior, he must protect the formula from being forgotten.[10] The scene is at once both absurd and realistic. Realistic because nothing which emerges from the unconscious into the light of the conscious adheres to conventions. Ideas appear when they want to, with no regard to whether or not the time is convenient. At the same time, important insights are often fleeting in nature. Like Carl Friedrich Gauß, we too have to quickly record important ideas and wrest them, as it were, from the unconscious in order that they do not disappear again into the darkness. Flashes of insight and inspiration such as these are evidence of the fact that the unconscious is always present and influences our consciousness as a shadowy background.

The metaphor of lamplight for our reflexive consciousness helps us to understand how different people are in a conscious and waking state and how they direct their consciousness against the background of the unconscious: some people are able to focus a bright, sustained and highly concentrated beam of lamplight onto a certain point, making them capable of intense concentration. Others tend to use a diffuse, widely scattered half-light. This dim light corresponds to that which we call free-floating attentiveness, and it allows people to be open to receiving images and impressions from the unconscious. In contrast to the dream state during sleep, we are able to actively and consciously release ourselves from such daydreams. Even when some people have little desire to detach themselves from the images of their unconscious and turn their attention to external tasks, they are able to do so if they make an effort. As long as we are awake, we are fundamentally able to change the direction and focus of our attention.

During sleep, this is no longer possible. As soon as we are exhausted or becoming tired, the lamp of our consciousness, metaphorically speaking, begins to dim by itself. Our capacity for attention and concentration gradually fades, as does our ability to think or perceive things. We can fight against this process for a while, but in the end, our lamp of consciousness extinguishes itself every night. Thus, we cannot switch the lamp of our consciousness on and off at will, as we can with a real lamp; we must abide by its own dynamics.[11] Yet sleep is neither a pitch dark state nor an uneventful one. We are able to experience quite a bit, and the experiences that we have are referred to as dreams.

Thus, while we are sleeping we are not completely unconscious; rather we possess a dream consciousness which is nevertheless different from our explicit consciousness.

Dream Worlds

In contrast to our daydreams, we are during our nighttime dream state not aware (except in exceptional cases) that the waking world exists. Generally speaking, only the dream world is recognizable and real to us while we are dreaming. Only when we awake are we able to distinguish between the two worlds: the waking world and the dream world. Some people consider the dream world to be an illusory world.[12] Opinions begin to differ as far as this perception is concerned. Can dreams be important and sometimes even helpful? Or like a fraudster, do they only cause us harm because they mimic reality and lead us to believe in something that does not exist?

At first glance, the actions and scenarios of many nighttime dreams do not seem deceptive, but in fact quite realistic. Within their own system of order, dream events can produce a completely logical story which could actually take place in the real world. It is only when we compare the dream and reality in detail that we often do discover a number of discrepancies. For example, in a dream, we may have a very close and familiar relationship with people with whom, in reality, we have been out of touch for many years. Furthermore, when our behavior within a dream differs significantly from our usual behavior in reality, we may perceive this as unrealistic. Then the dream does not reinforce the image that we have of ourselves, but presents us with unfamiliar or unimaginable facets of our personalities. This would be the case, for example, if we become physically violent in a dream even though in reality we would never engage in this kind of a conflict. It can also appear unrealistic to us if our home appears much more spacious in a dream than it is in reality, or if a stranger is living with us.

These few examples demonstrate that even dream narratives which are quite close to reality can already seem very fanciful from the point of view of the dreamer. And the borders between relatively realistic dreams and highly fantastical ones are fluid. Yet despite numerous similarities between dreams and reality, there are also significant differences. In a dream, we can go for a walk on the moon or fly above a forest like a bird, because a dream narrative does not have to obey the physical laws of our waking reality. We can meet a golden snake in the sky, a fairytale giant or a talking dragon in a dream, but not in reality. We meet these creatures only in dreams – and this is also true in the case of deceased people. The rules of time, with their strict ordering of past, present and future, are not binding in the dream world. For some people, the creative freedom found in dreams seems fascinating and exciting, whereas others see it as evidence that dreams simply lead us into meaningless, illusory worlds. Which of these two viewpoints is actually correct? And when is it worthwhile to delve into the subject of dreams?

The Possible Significance of Dreams

In Ancient Greece, dreams were believed to be a form of medicine for almost one thousand years. Sick people traveled to the temples of Asclepius, the god of healing, and lay down to sleep in the hope of being healed through a dream.[13] What sounds unimaginable or perhaps even beyond belief to us today was common practice at that time. At the ancient temple sites, countless stone tablets have been preserved to this day upon which people expressed their thanks to Asclepius for an act of healing. The Greek physician Hippocrates – originator of the medical oath that is still in use today – was likewise convinced of the importance of dreams. He believed that through dreams we can learn important things which are impossible to recognize in any other way. Hippocrates also maintained that the human soul can communicate the cause of an illness in a dream using the language of images.

Sigmund Freud brought this long-forgotten knowledge back to light in 1900 with his book *The Interpretation of Dreams* (German: *Die Traumdeutung*), thereby laying the groundwork for the interpretation of dreams in modern depth psychology. Freud had observed that dreams contained important information about the backgrounds of his patients' symptoms. Nevertheless, he had to admit that it is not easy to decipher the meaning of dream images. In his opinion, this incomprehensibility was the result of an internal psychological censorship which conceals our embarrassing wishes and emotions from us.

More recently, however, modern brain imaging examination methods have shown that something more like the opposite is true: dream images appear when our normal, waking censoring apparatus is shut down. In a waking state, certain areas of the brain located in the forehead area (frontal lobes) ensure that we are able to control, steer and discipline ourselves instead of reacting in a completely uninhibited and impulsive manner. It is exactly these areas which are inactive when we dream.[14] In our dreams we live, so to speak, in a more free and uncontrolled manner than we do in the waking state, because logically stringent and purposeful action moves into the background. This is also apparent in the fact that activities such as reading, writing and calculating, which require thought and reflection, occur only seldom in dreams – even among people who devote many hours to these activities during the day.[15]

What causes this extensive loss of our ability to exert control during our dreams? The path is made clear for unusual, surprising and bizarre occurrences. Dreams create and try out novel ideas. In a manner of speaking, our dreams play games with us and in the process, expose us to new experiences, adventures and emotions.[16] From this perspective, people who can cope well with disorder, unfamiliar circumstances or chaos are probably more open and receptive to their dream worlds than people who do not like to relinquish control and structure. However, given the complexity of life, we can scarcely avoid either chaos or order; rather, we must learn to deal with both of these conditions.

Dreams sometimes play out dire possible scenarios which we would not be able to tolerate well or overcome in our waking life. Thus, for example, a passionate amateur gardener dreamed that a horde of wild pigs were ransacking his garden; in the morning he was very relieved to find his garden undisturbed. His nightmare did not come true, but feeling of experiencing this kind of destruction remained with him. He tried out the sensation of anxiety, so to speak, in his dream. Similarly, a woman awoke with the need to immediately ensure that her friend was still alive because she had had a very realistic dream in which the other woman had a fatal heart attack. This dreamer sensed that her shocking dream was a kind of training in leave-taking. Dreams, however, play not only with terrible possibilities, but also with our wishes and desires; they may tell stories of a dream house or the man or woman of our dreams. Then, occasionally, we feel sorry to have to wake up and return to reality.

When and How do we Dream?

A person who is frequently plagued by bad dreams might wish for a dream-free life and perhaps look with envy at people who do not dream. Conversely, others find it a pity that the world of dreams remains closed to them. Is it possible that some people dream and others never do?

Since without memory, we have no access to our dreams, we must first clarify what our capacity for memory looks like. A representative survey of 1,000 Swiss men and women conducted in 1984 showed that only 6 percent never remembered their dreams. By contrast, 14 percent of those surveyed – that is, one out of every seven people – remembered their own dreams every morning.

Surveys conducted in other countries show similar results.[17]

However, the ability to remember dreams is not an unchangeable personality trait; rather, it is subject to certain fluctuations. For example, people's ability to remember dreams seems to be at its best during puberty, and it can increase again during periods of personal upheaval or identity crises. Creative or supposedly "thin-skinned" people often have an easy time remembering their dreams. Likewise, people who have trouble sleeping through the night and awaken frequently remember their dreams more often than people whose sleep is undisturbed. The more often a person wakes up, the more often he or she is able to capture the memory of her dreams. Modern sleep psychology research takes advantage of this phenomenon. Researchers allow people to go to sleep in a sleep laboratory and then wake them at precisely defined times and interview them about their dreams. However, this systematic examination of human dream activity has only been possible since the structure of our sleep was deciphered, approximately 90 years ago.

When the Jena psychiatrist Hans Berger first recorded the electric currents in the brain with an EEG (electroencephalogram), a device of his own invention, in 1924, it was only a matter of a few years before he was able to prove that human sleep is not a monotonous process, but is divided into five distinctive stages which repeat themselves in a rhythmic pattern over the course of the night.[18] Beginning with Sleep Stage 1 up until Stage 4, our sleep becomes increasingly deeper; at the same time, EEG frequencies become correspondingly slower and their amplitudes higher. Approximately 90 minutes after falling asleep, a healthy person generally moves into the fifth and last sleep stage for the first time: here, the brain begins to work more actively once again and is nearly awake. At the same time, activity increases in other systems of the body: pulse and respiratory rate rise, and blood flow to the genitals is intensified. The fast, jerky eye movements which can be detected in an electrooculogram (EOG) lend this sleep stage the name REM sleep. Less than 30 years after the discovery of the EEG, American researchers Eugene Aserinsky and Nathaniel Kleitman coined this term as an abbreviation for "Rapid Eye Movement" sleep. However, whereas numerous organs are demonstrably activated during REM sleep, electromyogram (EMG) testing shows that the body's muscle tonus drops sharply, with the result that a person in a state of REM sleep is scarcely capable of movement. Nature arranged this very sensibly, since neurobiological findings indicate that during our dreams we are not simply passive observers inside a "sleep cinema." In fact, imaging tests show that during dreamed activities, our brain activity is surprisingly similar to that seen during analogous activities which we actually perform.[19] If we were not incapable of movement during REM sleep, we would likely be able to act out our dream experiences unchecked.

The introduction of the three measurement techniques mentioned here – EEG, EOG and EMG – along with the identification of the stages of sleep, marked the beginning of the era of psychological research in sleep laboratories. In order to determine when and how people dream, in 1955 Eugene Aserinsky and Nathaniel Kleitman began waking their monitored, sleeping test subjects at specific times and immediately interviewing them about their dreams. When awakened during REM phases, over 80 percent of the subjects reported vivid, image-rich dreams. Significantly fewer dreams were remembered from Sleep Stages 1 through 4, the so-called non-REM stages. Compared with the REM dreams, these dreams were usually shorter and less intense, and instead of scenes, the respondents more often reported on having thoughts. However, later studies were able to prove that the differences between REM and non-REM dreams are much less substantial than originally thought. Systematic waking processes in the laboratory also suggest that all healthy people dream throughout all phases of sleep; it is simply the ability to remember dreams under everyday conditions which varies from one person to the next.[20]

Often, it is not particularly difficult to improve one's own ability to remember dreams. An open mind, curiosity and interest in the world of dreams already represent an important first step. If you then keep a notepad and pen or a dictation device next to your bed in order to record your dreams immediately upon waking, you will be amazed to find how many more dreams become accessible to you thanks to a positive attitude and these practical recording tools. For people who have not been able to remember their dreams well up to now, it is crucial to increase the degree of attentiveness to one's dreams. However, this takes time. If you lack the necessary time because the responsibilities of the coming day are already swirling through your head from the moment you wake up, you will scarcely be able to commit any energy to remembering your dream images. This leaves only weekends or vacation days: at these times you might find the necessary leisure that allows you to better turn your attention inward and uncover your dreams.

2. Why do we Dream – and What for?

Dreams and Mental Health

In the fall of 2012, in the context of preparing his 8- and 9-year-old pupils for their First Communion, a religion teacher wanted to explore the subject of death and dying with them. He took the children to visit a chapel and showed them the laid out body of a deceased woman. Several of the children reacted with nightmares after seeing the corpse.[21] When something unsettles us or stirs up our emotions – and an encounter with a dead or dying human being can certainly do this – our dreams may pick up on this subject. However, the same experience does not affect all the people who have it in the same way: following the encounter with death, only some of the children experienced nightmares. In other words, our reactions vary, and it may seem puzzling that violent, traumatic experiences do not necessarily trigger nightmares. Thus, for example, Nelson Mandela indicated in an interview that he was never troubled by nightmares during his incarceration on Robben Island.[22] Conversely, it also happens that people report having terrifying dreams even though their outer lives have been free of any terrible events. What, then, are the causes or the reasons for our dreams?

In their search for the factors that provoke dreams, countless researchers have attempted to influence dreaming in an experimental setting. Howard Roffwarg, for example, had his test subjects spend several days wearing glasses that colored their environment red. As a result, from night to night, their dream images became increasingly red in color. As soon as the test subjects stopped using the glasses the effect disappeared, and their dream images returned to the colors they had been before the experiment. Thus, there is a transfer of information between our waking impressions and the world of our dreams. But the question remains as to which of our daytime experiences find their way into our dreams. In pursuit of an answer, researchers showed their test subjects different films before they went to sleep – one with a light-hearted subject and one with a more distressing theme. Some of the scientists were subsequently frustrated that they had not identified any reliable criteria which could explain whether and how the content of a film would influence a subject's dream life in the following night. The connection between the images in the film and in people's dreams seems primarily coincidental.

However, in other experiments, certain correlations between waking content and dream content were recognizable. Test subjects who firmly resolve to dream about a subject which is personally highly significant to them before they go to sleep have the experience – not always, but more frequently than by random chance – that their dreams pick up on the theme in question.[23] Based on their scientific research in sleep laboratories, psychologists Inge Strauch and Barbara Meier confirmed that it is this subjective significance which is the determining factor: subjects which are highly emotionally relevant to us in real life appear in our dreams much more often than banal daily occurrences. Yet on the whole, dreams seem to select their subjects and images according to an unknown pattern. Whether and when a dream will pick up on a theme from daily reality – and especially, what story the dream will invent around it – still seems to be largely a mystery.[24]

Some researchers, not content to satisfy themselves with these vague results, examined whether external stimuli that we experience during sleep can influence our dreams. To this end, Inge Strauch and Barbara Meier exposed their sleeping subjects to the sound of a fighter jet or the sobbing cry of a human being.[25] Only one out of every three dreams appeared to have reacted to the stimulus, implying that influencing dreams directly is not so easily possible. Furthermore, it is unclear to what degree such results are subject to error: the dreams themselves could have integrated the sound into an image or a scene without this being recognizable. The researchers also noticed that the people analyzing the dreams – who did not know whether or to which sounds the dreamers had been exposed – sometimes made faulty associations: they assumed reactions to sound in cases where the subject had not been exposed to any sound; or they were unable to identify the correct sound, confusing the jet fighter with the crying sound.

In subsequent laboratory tests, other sense organs were stimulated: the sleeping subjects were exposed to touch,[26] odors, music or visual stimuli. Smells and visual stimuli had virtually no effect on dreams under laboratory conditions; being touched while sleeping had more influence. This is not surprising, since physical contact is rarely a completely neutral experience; it arouses feelings in waking people – be they pleasant or unpleasant. As an intimate experience, physical contact during sleep as well as in the waking state is not banal; it "gets under your skin."

On the whole, therefore, spontaneous observations and experimentally placed factors both point in the same direction: experiences[27] which are subjectively truly important to us or have an influence on us find their way into the images and scenarios of our dreams. This might explain why the same or very similar experiences are not integrated into the dreams of everyone who lives through them in the same way. But why is it, then, that we sometimes dream about banalities? In life as well as in dreams, there are always banal impressions which scarcely interest us or mean nothing to us at all. It is also conceivable, however, that our explicit consciousness experiences a certain thing as not very important, whereas from the perspective of our unconscious it is relevant. This would mean that the unconscious and the conscious mind have differing conceptions of a thing's importance. In addition, we are only capable of consciously perceiving a fraction of the information that bombards us on a daily basis. However, as already mentioned, information which escapes our conscious perception is not necessarily lost; rather, it may be stored unconsciously in our implicit memory.

This is clearly demonstrated by a dream which astonished a patient of the Swiss psychiatrist C. G. Jung. Shortly before he planned to sign a contract, he dreamed that while he was signing his name, his hand turned black. When he subsequently began a discreet investigation, it became apparent that he would, in fact, have "made his hands dirty" by signing the contract. For some people, this experience may seem to border on magic. However, if we assume – as Claparède and Sperry's abovementioned experiments on implicit memory imply – that we perceive things not only consciously but to a greater extent unconsciously as well and that we store our perceptions in our memory and can implicitly comprehend their meaning, then the dream about the blackened hand is quite logical and plausible.

Neuroscientific Findings

The sources of dreams, therefore, are often emotionally important and interesting subjects; this has also been confirmed through neuroscientific research. Modern imaging processes such as positron emission tomography (PET) or functional magnetic resonance imaging (fMRI) demonstrate that certain sections of the brain – the so-called limbic system – are highly active not only during dreams but also during the formation of so-called basic emotions.

From a spatial standpoint, dreaming and the four basic emotions take place within the same brain structures. The basic emotional control system includes those structures which support *rage, fear, panic* and the *seeking* system, which probably plays a key role in our dreams. The *seeking* system springs into action as soon as we are missing or lacking something. For example, when we are thirsty or hungry, the *seeking* system is active, just as it is when we have a desire for sex or become interested in a particular thing. As soon as the *seeking* system is activated, it releases the neurotransmitter dopamine.[28] In order to determine whether the *seeking* system actually plays a crucial role in the dreaming process, psychoanalyst Ernest Hartmann woke his healthy test subjects after their first REM phase and gave them either L-dopa[29] or a placebo. The individuals who received L-dopa remembered significantly more vivid, intense or bizarre dreams than those subjects who received either a placebo or no medication at all.

Dreaming also has a great deal to do with curiosity and exploration. When we dream, our psyche goes on a quest, as it were, and wants to find something. And that is actually possible – because when we dream, not only are those brain structures activated in which emotions are processed, but also areas which are responsible for the process of remembering. Stimulated by important experiences, the psyche searches through our stored reservoir of experiences and uses them to weave together dream images or entire dream scenarios. And since, as we have already pointed out, the psyche is much freer during our dreams than it is in the waking state, it permits itself to make connections and form patterns which we might sometimes reject if we were to view them from a rational or moral standpoint in a state of waking consciousness. The censor of our conscience, which is largely absent during sleep, allows the psyche to leave behind old or habitual life patterns and try out new options and possibilities. For this reason, some neurobiologists came to the conclusion that we dream primarily in order to solve our problems or develop new ideas.

Based on this assumption, dreaming would then be a very creative psychological process which has already existed for as long as 150 million years. This is the amount of time that mammals have populated the earth, and experimental evidence has proven that REM sleep occurs in all of the higher mammals. From the perspective of evolutionary biology, the dreaming process could scarcely have existed over such a long period of time if it did not constitute any advantage for the survival of the species and its adaptation to the environment. It is not only our mental activity during the "day shift" that has a meaning and a purpose, but the psychological processes during the "nightshift" as well.[30] In the dream state of the night shift, the psyche can deal, as it were, with those things that were left unattended during the day shift because they were forgotten or could not be processed. In this context, Wolfgang Kleespies compared the human brain with a bank: the operative day-to-day business is taken care of during the day; then, during the night shift, the psyche tests out new business strategies. To put it simply, strategies are always called for when there is a need to plan for the future. A strategist concerned with economics, for example, would examine the direction in which a business should go, which goals are worthwhile and what means can be employed to reach those goals. Thinking and acting strategically means looking toward the future. Someone who has an instinct for coming opportunities and potential – who can has a sense for what is lucrative or can "sniff" what is in the air – can be strategically successful. If, in fact, dreams contain strategic clues or can stimulate strategic thinking, they would then be a valuable resource in planning for the future.

Strategic Learning Through Dreams

One famous example in which a dream led to strategic considerations is the Pharaoh's dream in the Bible.[31] In his dream, the Pharaoh sees seven fat cows emerge from the Nile and graze in the reeds. A short time later, seven thin cows come up out of the Nile and devour the fat cows, yet they remain emaciated and ugly. In the following dream scenario, the Pharaoh must watch as seven parched ears of grain swallow up seven full, healthy ears, yet still remain puny. These dream images greatly trouble the mighty ruler; he wants to understand them and sends for Joseph, the interpreter of dreams. Joseph is able to build a bridge between the dream world and the waking world because he knows how to translate the metaphorical language of the dreams. Joseph explains that the two dreams are identical in terms of structure and content. At first, the Pharaoh sees abundance and prosperity in the flourishing animals and plants. Next, he sees life from the impoverished side: the animals and plants are severely emaciated. But these contrasting images are not simply standing peacefully side by side. The emaciated beings completely destroy the prosperity that originally existed. In the end, nothing is left but want and misery: it is a nightmare which, according to Joseph, points to the country's cyclical economic process. After seven years of abundance, seven years of famine will sweep across the land, and nothing of the original riches will remain.[32] Yet for Joseph, these dream images do not represent an unavoidable fate, but rather a danger which must be dealt with cleverly. His strategic foresight comes into play when he advises the Pharaoh to prepare for the time of need through smart economic policies. During the years of prosperity, he should raise taxes in order to fill the granaries in readiness for the years of famine. Joseph's idea won over the Pharaoh, and the grain reserves collected during the years of abundance were on hand years later when, indeed, a famine arose.

Thus, the Pharaoh's nightmare led to a policy-making decision: without the dream, he probably would not have taken any preventive measures for the future, but simply expected that growth and prosperity would continue. From a strategic standpoint, therefore, the question of "Why do we dream?" is less interesting than the question "What is the actual purpose of our dreams?" With a "why?" we are actually looking back into the past and searching for the cause of present-day developments. With a "what for?" on the other hand, we are looking primarily forward and wish to know the direction in which conditions or situations will develop.[33]

The Swiss psychiatrist C. G. Jung called for this kind of strategic viewpoint with regard to dreams at the beginning of the twentieth century when he argued in favor of analyzing dreams not only from a causal point of view but from a prospective one as well.[34] In a causal analysis, one searches for the root cause of the dream; in other words, one wants to find out which events in the near or distant past the dream is referring to and why. In a prospective examination, one is interested in the purpose for which the individual is having a particular dream. What does the dream want to accomplish? What is its goal or purpose? In the case of nightmares

30

in particular, it might be difficult to take this kind of dreamed intention into consideration. What is the purpose, for example, of a nightmare experienced by a very successful man who holds an executive position in which he sees the rear cars of a train going off the rails because the locomotive driver has raced out of the railway station at top speed?[35] The dream is a reminder of the dangers of high speeds. A person who drives too fast in the wrong location can cause a dire catastrophe. The purpose of this dream might be to advise the dreamer to examine the subject of speed and slowness in his own concrete life situation: am I living in the fast lane? Am I trying to get ahead too quickly? Or is a certain situation in danger of going "off the rails" because I want to implement it too hastily? These are not popular questions. If, in fact, they "hit the mark," a decision-making conflict arises: can I continue in the same way without concern, or would it be advisable to put the brakes on? What speed will be appropriate in the future? This dream invites the dreamer to make a prognosis. If he lays the tracks in the right way, with the right degree of sensitivity, perhaps he can improve his own mental health.[36]

Particularly during crises or difficult situations, dreams can have a healthy effect if we take their images into account when structuring our lives. A dream prognosis is similar to a weather prognosis, and human beings have been interested in both of these things since prehistoric times. Someone who is familiar with weather developments can prepare for them and plan certain things better; and a person who is familiar with the developmental tendencies of his or her psyche can prepare herself better. The advantage of this is that one can then orient oneself according to one's own individual mental state rather than relying on average values. After all, not every so-called workaholic needs to slow down her working pace, decrease her workload or change her lifestyle. A person's work-life balance may be right for him or her, even if she works very hard and lives unhealthily from a statistical point of view. However, if a dream tells you about a train derailment or shows you images of other dangers, it is worth taking a look at the state of balance in your own life. In order to live healthily, we require a physical and mental balance; we tend to lose this over and over, but we can always find it once again.

Dreams Contribute to Health

Our psyches seem to continually strive for physical and mental balance through self-regulation. What do we mean by this? At the physical level, we can observe the principle of self-regulation in our autonomic nervous system, with its sympathetic and parasympathetic branches. Whereas the sympathetic nervous system facilitates an overall increase in performance – and can therefore, upon demand, increase our heart-rate and blood pressure, mobilize glucose and improve blood flow to the muscles – its counterpart, the parasympathetic nervous system, slows these activities down. When we are active or under stress, the effects of the sympathetic nervous system are dominant; during periods of relaxation, the parasympathetic nervous system takes the upper hand. The vital opposing forces of exertion and relaxation work in constant alternation and as long as we are healthy, they constantly aim to balance one another out.

At the psychological level as well, there seems to be a drive toward equilibrium. For example, someone who goes to extremes in his or her conscious attitude toward life, whose lifestyle is very one-sided or psychologically unhealthy, may be confronted with dreams which are in vivid contrast to his own world view or reality. C. G. Jung referred to this tendency toward contrast in dreams as compensation. Thus, one man was surprised to find himself dreaming of a drunken vagrant wallowing in roadside ditch. Since he perceived himself as morally irreproachable, a dream like this seemed nonsensical.[37] However, when one considers the idea of compensation, these dream images could point to an aspect of the dreamer's personality which is in stark contrast to his unilaterally positive image of himself. The dream might, in fact, be asking: who are the people that you look down on in real life? And are you really a conscientious man through and through, or do you also

32

have a neglected side to your personality which you unconsciously despise? Or are you, perhaps, suppressing your fear of descending into the gutter?

In a similarly drastic manner, a woman dreamed that she was invited to an elegant social event. When the door was opened for her, she walked into a cowshed.[38] If dreams represent one's inner psychological truth and reality as they are at the moment, then the woman might realize that her friends are not only sophisticated, but might also sometimes be "stupid cows." This dream, too, draws something primitive into the dreamer's field of vision and thereby balances out the dreamer's one-sided admiration for the invited guests. Her positive viewpoint is supplemented by less attractive aspects.

But how can such images of unappealing human character-istics be helpful to a person's mental health? Do they not simple pull the dreamer into a harmful psychological quagmire? A per-son who dreams about a vagrant, a junky or a depraved person will be inwardly touched by something which, in his external life, he is perhaps familiar with only from the media. If dream images such as these inspire him to confront his own feelings of self-worth, he might gain a more realistic picture of his own strengths and weaknesses. In truth, every one of us has a self-worth complex. If we sit together in a group and spend some time discussing education, relationships, money, beauty or success, we will – whether consciously or unconsciously – assign ourselves a ranking value. And if we position ourselves very highly, we might feel excessively superior or overly secure. A dream about a vagrant could be a painful reminder that this is not completely true, and that something distasteful – or fear of the distasteful – also lives in all of us. Perhaps these or similar images will encourage us to make clear to ourselves how much of what we have in life is due to our personal accomplishments and how much is due to luck. A person who recognizes his or her good fortune will often become milder in her judgment of the fates of others, or less arrogant. However, dreams might not only speak to an exaggerated sense of self-worth, but to a low one as well. Sometimes we might feel too stupid, too small or too worthless, even if things are not going so badly for us. Thus, the woman who dreamed about the cowshed might consider whether her feelings of inferiority are based on the fact that she devalues herself too much in comparison to others, or perhaps even despise herself.

It would be incorrect if the two examples given above were to create the impression that a fixed meaning can be assigned to the dream motifs of "vagrant" or "cowshed." It is not possible to decipher the meaning of dreams if one is not familiar with the dreamer's life situation and without his or her thoughts or clarifications concerning the dream scenario. After all, compensation means that there may be a discrepancy – either large or small – between our consciousness and the unconscious which wants to balance itself out. Therefore, we can only unravel the meaning of a dream if we are able to compare the two aspects with each other – our conscious attitudes and our unconscious dream images.

Regardless of whether or not we consider dream messages to be helpful, dreaming does seem to be a biological phenomenon which supports our mental health. Several decades ago, researchers were already able to observe the adverse effects which occurred when they consistently disturbed their human subjects' REM sleep phases.[39] After approximately seven days of REM-sleep deprivation, many test subjects complained of nervousness, irritability or difficulty concentrating; immediately following the deprivation experiments, they experienced increased phases of REM sleep. This physiological need to catch up could be an indication that we require a certain amount of undisturbed REM sleep – and consequently, a certain amount of dreaming – in order to maintain our physical and mental balance.

These modern findings are not fundamentally new. According to Jewish tradition, a person is healthy when he or she can connect the hidden world with the world of appearances – that is, the unconscious dream world with concrete reality. Only through the connection between both of these halves of life and both of these realities can a person live wholly and completely – in other words, healthily.[40] This might also be what Reinhold Messner means when he says: "My life is a double one: I dreamed everything first, and then I lived it." He goes on to say: "Without dreams, there is no adventure. Booking an adventure – what nonsense. Adventures can neither be planned, nor copied, nor insured."[41] Like Reinhold Messner, we are all at home in two different worlds: in the conscious one and in the unconscious. And should we decide against having real adventures, we can still have them in our dreams; in our nightmares, we can even have terrible adventures which are a horror as well as a mystery to our consciousness.

Dreams Strike Where we are Most Vulnerable

What happens when we allow people to keep talking long enough? Then we almost always encounter complexes – subjects which trigger intense emotions. For example, if we speak long enough about money in a small group, we will touch upon our personal complexes related to money relatively quickly. After all, money is something which concerns all of us. We all have a personal relationship to money, an individual opinion and certain emotions. As soon a discussion of income, assets or taxes becomes heated, our complexes come into play. The same is true for emotionally-charged discussions over the family inheritance. In a discussion over inheritance, experiences of "not getting our fair share" which we thought we had overcome long ago, or sibling rivalries reaching far back into childhood, can become a topic all over again. Old parental and sibling relationships and experiences rise to the surface anew, and we are emotionally transported back into our mental past. We feel or behave the way we did in our childhood, even if we may not always be conscious of it.

As soon as we fall back into this type of childish relationship pattern, with its associated worries or conflicts, our parental and sibling complexes are at work, and in some cases we may not be able to control our inner feelings. Complexes are, so to speak, our sore spots; however, they are not pathological or harmful per se – they are a completely normal phenomenon. Everyone has them, just as everyone has a liver or a heart. As emotional organs, complexes only become a problem when we react in a childish manner even though this is no longer appropriate or necessary. Someone, for example, who was at the mercy of a sadistic father will often unconsciously expect all people in positions of authority to behave sadistically as well. However, this idea is a stereotype and it is incorrect. And even if we are confronted with a sadistic authority figure at some time in our lives – which certainly could happen – we are no longer a small, helpless child.

Complexes not only constantly influence our waking life (whether consciously or unconsciously), they also appear frequently in our dreams.[42] Particularly during times of crisis in our lives or when we need to make important decisions, dreams play with our established complex patterns, interlink them in new ways or expand them through new perspectives. When a 30-year-old man – I will call him Stefan – was toying with the idea of finally moving out of the apartment he had been sharing with his divorced mother, he was surprised to have the following dream:

> My mother and my aunt are sitting in our kitchen, and I join them. Mother tells both of us that she wants to move away because she has been offered an attractive job in Frankfurt. I have tears in my eyes, but I don't want anyone to see them, so I leave the kitchen. I am shocked.

Up to now, Stefan had not dared to move into an apartment of his own because he was convinced that his mother would not be able to deal with being alone. At the same time, he was annoyed that he was still living at home and at such close quarters with his mother. He felt controlled, and her involvement in his life got on his nerves. Discussions usually ended with mutual accusations and a tense atmosphere. But now the dream seemed to turn Stefan's beliefs on their heads. The impulse to change their life situation came not from him, but from his mother. And it was not his mother who reacted with sadness to the approaching separation. This dream made it possible to question his previous view of his mother, himself and their relationship. Had he gone too far in reducing his mother to her maternal role and not wanted to acknowledge that she might now be a woman who had plans for her own future? Had he failed to recognize that she might be attracted to a life free of responsibility for a child? Stefan was five years old when his father left the family and completely broke off contact. For a long time, he was aware of what a catastrophe the separation represented for him and his mother. They clung to each other and gave each other comfort and stability. In the dream, the imminent separation is no longer a catastrophe for his mother – probably because she is not looking back at the losses experienced in her life up to now, but is looking forward toward her future possibilities. This kind of attitude makes it easier to take steps toward change. Stefan, on the other hand, is confronted with his own potential sorrow, of which he had not been aware up to now. Instead, his waking life is dominated by resentment and irritation. It is difficult for him to imagine that he might be overwhelmed by the separation, because he is flooded by feelings of sadness that he does not dare to let show.

Through the dream, Stefan became aware of his own area of vulnerability. His desire for an independent life was overshadowed by his parents' separation and the associated painful emotions of which he had scarcely been aware up to now. The dream images made it possible for him to see his situation in a new light and to reevaluate his fear of making a change.

3. What are Nightmares?

Ancient Myths and Neurobiological Insights

A nightmare is a kind of intruder. It disturbs our peace of mind by confronting us with upsetting images which terrify us and wake us up. In our nightmares, we have terrible experiences. These dreadful things happen to us not externally, but in our inner life. There is scarcely any room there for beauty, joy or pleasure. And nightmares which reveal something evil and significant for an entire age – like the Pharaoh's dream in the Bible – can even become part of our cultural heritage.

The emotional impact of a nightmare not only prevents us from forgetting it quickly; it also triggers numerous physical stress reactions, such as a racing heartbeat, shortness of breath or even feelings of suffocation. It can even happen that we wake up with a scream, drenched in sweat, or with the feeling of being paralyzed. On the other hand, a nightmare can get us up out of bed because we want to stay awake in order not to keep dreaming. Sometimes we feel compelled to get up because we want to make certain that everything in the concrete world is all right. And if we dread being alone with the terrible dream images, we might wonder whom we could confide in and share the story. Nightmares do not seem to spare any small section of our humanity; rather, they assault us at every level. Internal images, emotions, our physical bodies and our external reality are all affected. In this sense, there is a totalitarian aspect to nightmares.

When someone tells us about nightmare images of being chased or raped, or of falling into a bottomless abyss, we can usually sympathize easily with their fear and consternation. Situations like this are traumatic for everyone. However, there are also dream experiences whose menacing nature is not immediately perceptible or obvious from the outside. Thus, in his dream, a young man went into a panic because he was unable to glue on the broken pin for locking the door on the driver's side of his car. He woke up with a racing heartbeat, trembling all over his body, and felt weak for days afterward. His best friend could not comprehend this dreamed panic: after all, it was simply a technical problem which could hardly be repaired by gluing, but could be easily fixed by a competent professional. However, the question of whether or not a dream constitutes a nightmare cannot be decided by an outside person, but only by the dreamer him or herself. It is the subjective physical and emotional experience which makes a dream a nightmare. Since only the dreaming person himself experiences the fear during the nightmare and upon awakening, he is the only person who can ultimately evaluate the intensity and quality of the terror.

Nevertheless, as a rule, only nightmares that occur during REM sleep contain images or scenes which we are able to remember well. Sleep laboratory experiments have shown, however, that nightmares or frightening dreams can occur not only during REM sleep, but during Sleep Stages 2 and 4 as well.[43] A person who experiences a nightmare during the deep sleep of Stage 4 will usually wake up screaming and seem confused or very upset. The dreamer experiences pure, naked fear, because in most cases people cannot remember any dream content from this stage of sleep. Whatever it was that triggered the fear is immediately forgotten and remains shrouded in darkness. Therefore, the dreamer cannot pinpoint or classify his or her fear; it remains nameless and faceless. As long as we are unaware of the background or root cause of our fear, we can neither explain it nor can we consider how we might be able to control it. We can hardly imagine ourselves in a more helpless or threatened position. This kind of fear can only be counteracted through a feeling of security. This might come from a person who takes us in his or her arms and stays with us while we have to endure the fear. However, internal images or the power of faith can serve as a counterbalance to fear and provide us with support.

A Greek Myth Explains the Origin of Nightmares

One of the most famous paintings by the Zürich-born artist Henry Fuseli (German: *Johann Heinrich Füssli*) is entitled "The Nightmare." The picture, produced around 1780, depicts a beautiful young woman lying on her back on a sofa with her arms outstretched. She wears a delicate, cream-colored negligée. It is nighttime, and she appears to be sleeping. An erotic tension hangs in the air. Crouching on her torso is a hairy, gnome-like creature. The two figures are not alone; rather, they are observed by a horse with penetrating, glassy eyes. The horror of the nightmare is animalistic in nature.

Fuseli's painting picks up on an image which extends back to ancient times. In the past, people were convinced that nightmares were caused by a demon that sits on the sleeping person's chest and steals the air that he or she breathes. In the German-speaking world, the creature was called *Alp* or *Alb*; in the Netherlands, it was called *Mahr*. Both of these terms have been preserved up to the present day, in the German word *Albtraum* and the English term "nightmare."[44]

This nightmare demon was frequently portrayed in the form of a thickset, human-like being. He usually had long, shaggy hair and a haunting expression. The images resemble the Greek god of nature, Pan, who in Antiquity was believed to be the perpetrator not only of panic, but also of nightmares. Pan was said to have sent salacious or frightening dreams to people who sought peace and protection in the shadows during the heat and humidity of midday. Pan was a mixed creature – half human and half goat. His body and face were human, but he walked on goat's legs and had two horns. His tousled hair and unkempt beard emphasized his wild nature.

As a symbol, Pan gives us hints about the origins of panic and nightmares. According to legend, he liked to prowl around dark caves, near water or under trees. He loved nature in its primordial, wild state. As soon as Pan appeared in the vicinity of cultivated fields and civilized human settlements, the people reacted with fear and distress – that is, with "panic." Yet Pan was not a malicious goblin or an enemy of culture. He did not antagonize the people; he was simply strange and foreign to them.

Human panic, therefore, is rooted in the awareness of unbridled natural forces, as they existed prior to all human cultures and as they continue to exist today alongside every culture. This nature dictates the rules of the game, to which all living things are subject. Only culture and civilization have freed us human beings from this helplessness to a certain degree – both with respect to the natural outside world that surrounds us as well as to our internal psychic and autonomous physical processes. We long ago ceased to depend on the spontaneous, unreliable gifts of nature; we now cultivate fields and raise animals. We are not exclusively at the mercy of our desires and moods; rather, we can discipline ourselves to concentrate and focus on a task. Physical or mental illnesses are not a fate we must simply accept: they can be mitigated or healed through medical treatment, psychotherapy and medication. Thanks to technology and culture, we are becoming increasingly independent from the laws of nature.

Yet whenever Pan appeared to the ancient Greeks, they were reminded that human-created order and culture are fragile, and they are only one aspect of life. This also became very apparent in the case of sexuality, which Pan lived out spontaneously. Pan acted on his desires with abandon, freely and without regard for consequences. Moral laws or marital fidelity – cultural inventions – meant nothing at all to him. Interestingly, in the late Middle Ages, Pan served as a template for depictions of the Devil. Externally, the relationship between the two beings is easily recognizable. Both the Devil and Pan are depicted with horns and goat's hooves. Both of them love pleasure, lasciviousness and desire. This fascinates people, yet it frightens them at the same time. From a psychological standpoint, one could say that everything which has been demonized since the Middle Ages – everything that arouses desire and escapes control – can also create panic and trigger nightmares. In this way, panic and nightmares can be seen as the flipside of our archaic impulses.

Mythologically speaking, Pan manifests himself at the latest in periods of transition, when an entire culture breaks down. Pan – and along with him panic, inner nightmares or concrete, external ones – seems to be associated with borderline experiences. Panic occurs at the border between human culture and animalistic nature, and this may be experienced by a single individual or by an entire society. We might think that ancient myths such as these are only chronicled in books. But this is not true: they also lie buried in the depths of our memories. Thus, our unconscious reservoir of experience extends far beyond our individual lives. Therefore, our inner images or fantasies may be completely personal, but they may also draw on symbols from long-forgotten mythology.

The close connection that still exists today between panic and wild nature is demonstrated in the images created by a young woman. When she had a sudden panicked reaction during a therapy session, she attempted to illustrate her panic in a sandplay image. Sandplay is a non-verbal therapy method in which clients can create scenes using small figures in a sand tray.[45] The woman chose a crocodile, a snake, a dinosaur and the "hellhound" Cerberus, and placed them in the corners of the sand try. For her, this was the best possible depiction of her inner psychological state. There was no need to add anything more. Panic could be demonstrated through wild animals which cannot be tamed by human beings. The guardian of the underworld and the realm of the dead was an element of her panic as well. Panic, therefore, arises in our encounters with natural energies which we cannot domesticate or control. This corresponds to the statement about the ancient myth of Pan.

But what can we do when Pan confronts us with panic or nightmares? Hermes, the herald of the gods is said to have conceived Pan together with the beautiful nymph Dryope.[46] After the birth, when

3. What are Nightmares? Ancient Myths and Neurobiological Insights

his mother saw her newborn child with his goat's hooves, horns and bearded face for the first time, she was horribly shocked. She ran away in panic and abandoned her son. Pan, therefore, was a lost, abandoned child. He would have been forsaken and died had his father, Hermes, not wrapped him lovingly in a rabbit skin and taken him in. If we translate this mythical scene psychologically, it could mean that Hermes has a nature which is capable of dealing with Pan. Instead of fleeing from Pan, he can turn towards him. Through Hermes' personality traits, mythology provides us some clues to emotional resources that can be helpful in dealing with nightmares and panic.

A quick first glance at Hermes, the messenger of the gods, tells us that he was not born to be a hero.[47] He was very aware of this, and therefore he never let himself become involved in aggressive confrontations. Victory in battle was not an option for him. Nevertheless, he was not without success. Thanks to his cleverness and cunning, he was able to overcome difficult challenges. He was capable of dealing masterfully with anything unexpected or unpredictable. He promptly and unconcernedly seized upon any unexpected valuable discovery or sudden luck in love. He was a master of the present moment; he never let a favorable opportunity pass him by unused. However, surprising gains go hand in hand with sudden losses. Whereas Hermes could lead one person to riches in the blink of an eye, another would be reduced to beggary. Hermes led people to treasure, but also to ruin. He was able to rejoice over a desired object, but he could also tolerate disappointment. He was familiar with the beautiful and pleasant aspects of the world as well as the dark and destructive ones. He was no stranger to human failings such as envy, hate or greed. In other words, he was acquainted with the entire spectrum of life, and he knew that the opposing forces of good and evil always work in alternation and exist in mysterious balance.

Hermes teaches us that when faced with panic and nightmares, we are not called upon, first and foremost, to activate our heroic side. Nightmares and panic are not adversaries or enemies which we must defeat in battle. Instead, it is to our advantage to prepare ourselves for spontaneous and unexpected events. Dangerous situations will always exist, and a person who is able to act cleverly and skillfully will have an advantage. Hermes, who is considered to be the inventor of language, also reminds us of the helpful significance of words. If we are able to express our terrible experiences in the waking or dreaming worlds, we can bring about a change. When a person tells others about his or her nightmares, or writes them down, she will find that the turmoil in her soul already becomes calmer. As an instrument of culture, language makes it possible to bring order to what we have experienced; our experience becomes communicable, so we can share it with others. We do not have to remain alone with the experience, and that can give us support. Sometimes, however, language is not the appropriate instrument – either because there are no words, or because words fail us. As the inventor of the lyre, Hermes could point out that music can also be helpful in dealing with terrifying experiences. In Ancient Greece, this idea was widespread: music was generally believed to have the power to heal illnesses.

Neurobiological Insights into Fear and Panic

Music can influence us very subtly, it can move us deeply, or it can also disturb us. It affects our moods and emotions.

Technically speaking, an emotion is a perception that is directed inward. When we experience grief, for example, we are very subjectively aware of our personal inner condition. The same is true for joy, anger and other feelings. For example, when a large dog makes us feel afraid, this emotion represents our personal, psychological reaction to the dog. In everyday speech, we do not always precisely differentiate between fear and panic; however, the experiences of fear and panic have different qualities, and they operate through different neurological pathways and messenger substances. Research into the basic emotions mentioned above has shown that *fear* and *panic* are biologically distinct systems. The central location for processing fear in the brain is the so-called amygdalae (Latin: *corpus amygdaloideum*). These are located on both sides in the middle of each temporal lobe. When people exhibit injuries in both amygdalae, they can experience neither fear nor anxiety. A condition which may seem enviable at first glance, is – when we examine it more closely – not necessarily advantageous. In its function as a warning signal fear can, in fact, function as a trigger for meaningful action.

Like all emotions, fear is linked to a physical reaction which is set in motion via hormones, neurotransmitters and other messenger substances. Fear can either stimulate a flight reflex, or it can cause us to freeze due to a "play-dead" reflex. As soon as a situation evokes fear in us, there are two possible scenarios within the brain: an extremely rapid process circumvents our consciousness and ensures that in dangerous situations we do not stop to consider our actions but simply act instinctively.[48] The second, and slower path for processing fear functions via the hippocampus, a structure in the brain which is responsible for our episodic memory. When our fear is processed through this second channel, we can call up our memories and consciously reflect on what is happening as well as comparing possible courses of action. But this takes time – and when quick action is necessary, instinct is the better option. After all, statistically speaking, instinct has proven its effectiveness for millions of years. We could describe instinct as a typical response to a typical life situation.

We are familiar with the two different possible reactions to fear[49] from our waking life – but also from our dreaming lives. Anyone who instinctively pulls a small child away from a cliff and prevents him or her from falling down – whether in a dream or in reality – is reacting effectively. But someone who – whether in reality or in a dream – instinctively swims with all his might in the direction of the shore should know that it is usually wiser to swim parallel to the beach; one's chances of reaching land are actually better this way. When we are afraid, either instinct or conscious knowledge, skill and competence may be called for.

From a neurobiological standpoint, *panic* is a completely different phenomenon from fear. The panic system is also called the *abandonment* panic system. As soon as it is stimulated, a person may not only experience panic attacks; he or she might also develop feelings of anguish, depression or loss.

This process is controlled by the hormones oxytocin and prolactin and by opioids. Oxytocin is always at work during childbirth. By stimulating contractions, it sets the birth process in motion; oxytocin also causes muscle contractions in the mammary glands which allow a mother to nurse her newborn child. However, oxytocin can do much more. Functioning as a counterpart to cortisol in regulating stress, it decreases our stress reactions by lowering our blood pressure and heart rate. Every pleasant skin-to-skin contact – be it a comforting massage or warmth – leads to the release of oxytocin and thereby influences our emotions. Feelings such as affection, love and trust, as well as every form of emotional attachment are reinforced through oxytocin. Furthermore, under the influence of oxytocin, we seem to be able to conduct difficult conversations more calmly.[50] The hormone prolactin works in a similar manner. At the physical level, it stimulates milk production in the mother; at the emotional level, it increases her readiness to care for and protect the newborn child. Prolactin can also be described as a nesting hormone; prolactin levels already begin increasing in pregnant women shortly before they give birth. These levels also rise in their partners, albeit significantly less than in the expectant mother. Nature seems to want to ensure that a newborn child will not be neglected.

In young mammals,[51] the panic system is activated when their mothers leave them alone for a certain length of time. The separation triggers panic, with the result that the level of endogenous opioids[52] decreases. Since endogenous opioids also act as pain reducers, separation and loss are painful – not only emotionally, but physically as well. Thanks to this panic system, young animals stay close to their mothers. In some autistic children the opioid system seems to be overactive. Due to their increased levels of opioids, they appear to experience much less pain when separated from an attachment figure than "average" children do.

What is panic, then, in light of the biological and emotional processes we have described? Most likely, panic is caused by the loss of attachment and security. As long as we experience ourselves as being supported and attached, we do not become panicked. Panic arises when we experience ourselves as existentially abandoned, unprotected or lost. In a state of panic, we are psychologically like a helpless child who misses his or her strong, nurturing mother. And this state applies to many nightmares. In nightmare scenarios, we frequently experience ourselves not only as threatened, but also abandoned and overwhelmed. We are not protected or comforted, either by others or within ourselves.

These neurobiological findings form a bridge to the Greek myth of Pan described above. Neurobiology and mythology do not contradict each other; rather, they both point in the same direction. After all, Pan had a mother problem: his mother ran away and abandoned him. The myth is told in the context of abandonment. Broken-off relationships, the pain of separation and helplessness are the pillars of the archetypal area in which panic arises.[53]

According to this logic, everything that strengthens strong attachments and feelings of security – and continues to function when a person is alone or under stress – can have a preventive or protective effect against panic and nightmares. Many small children feel sufficiently comforted when they are alone if they can hold onto a cuddly toy or a security blanket. But the older we become, the greater becomes the importance of internalized or immaterial "objects" which are capable of stabilizing us when we visualize or imagine them. An unusual custom practiced by an East African tribe demonstrates that music can be the source of this type of lifelong supportive power.[54] Here, the day of a person's birth is counted as the day that the mother hears, inside herself, the song of the child she wants to conceive. After she recognizes the song, she sings it together with her husband while they make love; they invite the child to join in with them. During her pregnancy, the mother sings the song from time to time, and during the birth, the midwives sing with her. Ultimately, all the residents of the village learn the newborn child's song, in order to sing it on important occasions in his or her life – the last time on the person's deathbed. This unique, personal song holds the individual's entire life together.

Nightmares in the Daytime and Nightmares at Night

When a myth or a fairy tale tells of a mother, this is meant to be understood symbolically. Here, "mother" does not simply mean the literal figure of a mother, but rather, everything in this world which can provide nourishment, care and warmth and thereby support someone's development. Thus, in war, all that is maternal is systematically destroyed. An individual mother may fight like a lioness for her children's survival – but at an overall level, in war, people are increasingly robbed of everything they need to survive. Their lives are constantly threatened. War is an external nightmare which systematically annihilates the experience of security.

Such concrete traumatic experiences leave emotional traces behind. The child and adolescent psychiatrist Reinhard Schydlo,[55] who was born during the Second World War, reports that he cannot remember of the terrible nights of bombing in the air-raid shelter or his family's escape. However, he has not forgotten the nightmares he experienced after the end of the war. Until well past the age of five, he was repeatedly jolted awake by falling dreams in which he plummeted to endless depths. With the increasing outer security that his family was able to find during the period after the war, his nightmares also came to an end. Even though Reinhard Schydlo remembered his own war experiences only from his parents' stories, they had found their way into his dreams.

Interestingly, nightmares can even draw on experiences and impressions extending back to our prenatal life in our mothers' wombs. Stress or emotional burdens that a mother experiences during her pregnancy do not leave the fetus unscathed; the unborn child perceives them and processes them emotionally. A phenomenon that pediatricians and therapists have been describing for decades has now been confirmed through neurobiology. The limbic system, which is responsible for the processing of emotions, begins developing as early as the sixth week of pregnancy. Therefore, an unborn child can process its experiences emotionally and store them unconsciously from a very early point in time.

Yet nightmares can even recall events that took place before we ourselves were conceived. Memories of trauma suffered during war that appear in nightmares reaching across generations demonstrate that information can be stored transgenerationally in the unconscious. Nor are the terrors of our ancestors' world forgotten forever. Our individual psyches call upon an ancient one – the collective psyche of humankind – which can show itself to us in dreams. We learn about this, for example, in Philippe Grimbert's[56] autobiographical novel, *Secret* (French: *Un Secret*): as a small boy, he experienced many terrible nights. He often slept restlessly and was tormented by nightmares in which an older brother appeared – one he did not actually have in reality – and he shed many tears. As soon as he went to bed and turned out his light, his tears began to flow – even though he did not know what to attribute them to. In addition, every night he was plagued by baseless feelings of shame and guilt. It was not until he was 15 years old that Louise, a close friend of the family, told him about the fate of his Jewish family. His half-brother – with whom he fought and argued repeatedly both in his nighttime dreams and in his daydreams – had actually existed, but was deported to Auschwitz.

Philippe Grimbert's inner images were, in fact, not an invention of his own; rather, they recalled real events which had occurred several years before his birth. And the revelations made by his friend Louise had a real effect: he felt stronger in his waking life, and his nights were different as well. Once he knew about his brother's existence and his name, there were no more struggles and no more nightmares. Figuratively speaking, the disclosure of the family secret created a bridge between his mental images and the real events of the past. Now that the connection between the dreaming and waking worlds had been made visible, his mind and spirit could be at rest. Philippe Grimbert's experience shows how helpful it can be when truths are revealed and named and connections are made visible. When things can be ordered in their proper place, we no longer feel confused or crazy.

We can see, then, that the nighttime world of dreams and the concrete daytime world have a reciprocal influence on each other. The torrent of images and emotions flows from the unconscious into the consciousness and vice versa. In people we might call "thin-skinned," this back-and-forth flow of images seems to occur with particular frequency and intensity. The borders between their interior and exterior worlds – as well as between their unconscious and conscious worlds – seem to be particularly porous. In this sense, we can look at the quality of being "thin-skinned" as a genetically determined constitutional openness and sensitivity.

However, a character trait such as this is not necessarily fixed for a lifetime; it can also be dependent on the specific conditions of our lives. For example, people who see themselves as robust and not highly susceptible to fantasies or dreams may very well become more open to them in crisis situations. Regardless of whether we want them to or not, the gateways between the unconscious and the conscious are most likely to swing open when we feel ourselves to be vulnerable or disoriented. Thus, for example, a fear of losing control in our own lives is often a trigger for nightmares. With this in mind, even a pregnant woman's fear of being at the mercy of the natural process of childbirth can become a subject for nightmares. Of course, the fear of complications during the birth or abnormalities in the child can also influence the dreams of pregnant women.

In every age group, there seem to be typical fears and insecurities which may flow into our nightmares. In a survey of 300 children[57] in his child and adolescent psychiatry practice, Reinhard Schydlo discovered nightmare subjects that were gender specific. Girls dreamed about embarrassment or humiliation or the loss or death of a loved one more often than boys did. More frequently than the girls, boys dreamed about overwhelming mountains of homework or conflicts within school – particularly if they suffered from attention deficit disorders.

People who suffer from nightmares anew or for the first time at an advanced age often find themselves confronted with long-forgotten experiences. The unconscious seems to be interested in events from the distant past, and it opens the door to memory. Here, an unhappy love affair, a devastating loss or a false decision may return to our consciousness rather than continuing to be repressed. The border between consciousness and the unconscious appears to be more porous when, because of age or other limitations, we become less involved in external activities. As soon as our external lives become somewhat slower or quieter, our inner, emotional world can move closer to the threshold of our consciousness and make the memories of our dreams more vivid. A similar phenomenon occurs in people who suffer from migraines only on the weekend, even though they work hard all week and remain symptom-free. The symptoms arise only when they are relaxed: this is what we call a release regression. Reduced stress levels experienced on weekends, during vacation time or upon retirement are therefore critical for some people, since they are particularly susceptible to illness at these times.

Anesthesia, Surgery and Organ Transplantation

Drugs can also increase permeability between the unconscious and conscious worlds. Medications such as the anesthetic ketamine function in the same vein. This substance is known for its psychotropic effects; among other things, it can trigger distorted perceptions as well as nightmares. In medical terms, we speak of a "brief reactive psychosis" when a medication or some other physical process induces a temporary psychotic disorder. Following lengthy surgeries, approximately ten percent of patients complain of psychological symptoms such as mood swings, agitation and disturbances in memory or concentration. These may be accompanied by disturbed sleep and nightmares which frequently deal with massacres, lynching situations or gang rape. In addition to the administered medication and temporary imbalances in the individual's metabolism, these are most likely also the result of psychological stress. Frightening fantasies experienced prior to an operation, as well as mental impressions after waking up, function as stressors which can intensify dream activity.

It is therefore not surprising that nightmares can also occur following organ transplantations. In this case however, in addition to the psychotropic factors mentioned above, other phenomena seem to be at work which up to now have not been widely recognized and have received little attention. Occasionally, dreams experienced following an organ transplant pick up on themes which have nothing to do with the organ recipient, but rather with the organ donor. In our dreams, therefore, we seem not only to be able to remember the experiences of our ancestors, as mentioned above; our dreams may also extend across the boundaries of individual persons. Thus, a few months after receiving a heart transplant, the dancer Claire Sylvia[58] not only experienced new dietary preferences and interests, but she also dreamed about a young organ donor. Her research confirmed that she had actually received the heart of her 18-year-old "dream man," and that she seemed to have "inherited" certain habits from him. The American cardiologist Paul Pearsall[59] observed a similar phenomenon. In approximately ten percent of heart transplant recipients, he recorded behavioral similarities with the respective donors, even though the recipients knew nothing about the deceased individuals. According to psychology professor Gary Schwartz, such phenomena could be an indication that our memory is anchored not only in the brain but also in the cells of our bodies. If this is correct – and there is a great deal of evidence to support it – the transplantation of a heart would not only be accompanied by its associated cellular memory, but also by those things that were "close to the heart" of the donor.

The US Army intelligence service, the *Intelligence and Security Command* also studied psychic influences extending across great distances. White blood cells were extracted from test subjects, placed in test tubes and moved up to 75 meters away from the subjects. While the test subjects were made to watch videos containing scenes of violence, the white blood cells reacted. It is actually inconceivable that blood cells which have been removed from the body would be able to maintain a connection to their donors. Perhaps quantum physics will be able to provide the key to understanding such processes. The Einstein-Podolsky-Rosen or EPR paradox[60] is a quantum mechanical thought experiment which addresses this problem. It describes two elementary particles which are initially connected to each other within a system but which then move far apart from one another. Strangely, however, the separated particles are not independent from each other. The measured value of one particle always supplements the measured value of the second particle, so that the exact same total value is repeatedly achieved. Despite physical distance, the two particles remain strongly correlated.

Is this believable – and what should we make of it? We have arrived at a point beyond the limitations of our ability to perceive and understand, where we are dealing with belief and disbelief as well as with wonder, fear and even awe. Nightmares can also penetrate into this otherworldly realm when they confront us with bizarre phenomena, chaos or demons or show us confusing or fragmentary images. This type of incomprehensible image is often impossible to communicate; the words fail us. The things that appear to us in dreams are neither explainable nor comprehensible and they evade every attempt at categorization. We search in vain for structures and patterns. It seems as if we have come into contact with that which people once called the hereafter or "the other side." These nightmares remind us of paintings by such artists as Max Ernst and Hieronymus Bosch. Anyone who recognizes his or her dream visions in their works or in those of others will not be left alone with her fears.

4. Dealing with Nightmares:

Discovering, Exploring and Understanding Yourself

While antidepressants have been shown to be ineffective in the treatment of nightmares, actively addressing the problem often appears to be beneficial. In the case of a 5-year-old boy, for example, the psychologist Michael Schredl[61] observed how quickly a conscious confrontation with the dream images can change a nightmare scenario. In his nightmares, the boy was threatened by ghosts, shadows and terrible monsters. Immediately after waking, he called for his mother and was usually unable to fall asleep again for several hours. When his therapist encouraged him to draw, he depicted the way, in his nightmares, his little dream ego stood face-to-face with two giant ghosts. When asked what could help him in facing his fear, he drew a large spider between himself and the menacing ghosts. Thus, the boy was not looking for a direct confrontation or fight with the threatening figures; instead, he built himself a kind of protective barrier. The spider was able to deal with the two ghosts. A spider – a creature feared by many children as well as adults – was capable of frightening off the ghosts or holding them at bay. In an action analogous to the principle of homeopathy, he treated like with like. In his drawing, the boy found his own personal, creative response to the dream. By further developing the frightening dream images, he also changed his own emotional equilibrium. Even though he remembered thematically similar nightmares one year later, he felt significantly less burdened by them. His nightmares became less frequent, and when he awakened he was able to fall asleep again on his own. Nevertheless, he insisted that his mother continue to record his dreams in his dream diary, and in his drawings he continued to playfully reshape the dream scenarios. Thus, he retained the behavior which had proven to be effective.

A person who instinctively feels a resistance to writing down or drawing his or her dreams might ask why he should want to record something that he doesn't want to look at but would rather be rid of. After all, writing or drawing objectifies the nightmare experience and makes it visible to the outside world. So isn't it more likely that our fears will be doubled now that our inner nightmare images are placed concretely in front of us and made real for ourselves or for others? Experience shows that in fact, exactly the opposite occurs. The act of illustrating our dream images frequently has a calming effect on our emotions. As soon as our dreams are documented in one form or another, they no longer seem to have such an overwhelming effect on our inner beings.

When dealing with nightmares, it is crucial to determine what is effective – regardless of whether a certain approach is helpful or plausible for others. Whatever works is correct. And according to C. G. Jung, if we carry a dream around with us for a long enough time, something will always come out. If we keep the dream with us, at some point we will be able to make sense of it in some way. What then emerges, however, may not necessarily be a scientific result that we can boast about or rationalize; but rather a sign or hint from the unconscious as to what direction our life's journey may take. Thus, the primary goal of dealing with our own dreams is to restore the positive flow of our lives.[62]

What is Dream Interpretation?

According to the Talmud, a dream which is not interpreted is an unread letter.[63] Based on this metaphor, interpreting a dream would be equivalent to reading a message. However, we can only read a letter or a message if we can recognize and understand the symbols of its language. Yet the language of dreams seems to be a phylogenetically ancient one – namely, the language of allegories and parables[64] whose meanings are not always obvious. Thus, we could define dream interpretation as the deciphering of a difficult-to-read text – which, in addition, often has not just one single meaning, but is in fact ambiguous and multi-layered.

Yet before a letter can even be read by its recipient, it must first of all be written and sent. Writing and reading letters is a multi-stage phenomenon. When writing a letter, we search for the appropriate ways to formulate our concerns and feelings. And we do not always put a finished letter in the mail.[65] But if we do send it, the recipient can then decide whether he or she wants to read it, lay it in a drawer unopened, or even throw it in the wastebasket. Thus, the dialogue which was intended when the letter was written may potentially come to a standstill at various levels.

When we transpose these everyday experiences onto the phenomenon of dreaming, the various levels at which dreams are effective become clear to us. As long as we do not remember our dreams at all, the dream-letter – metaphorically speaking – has never been sent. However, the mere fact that a "dream-letter" was written at all makes an impact. As we have already explained, through their very existence, dreams contribute to our psychological and physical health in a variety of ways. Therefore, even if we cannot or do not want to interpret our dreams, the fact that we have dreamed them is beneficial. But those of us who do not simply want to leave it at that will – to return to the same metaphor – open the dream-letter and read it. Dream interpretation, then, means attempting to find an answer for our unconscious images and cultivating a dialogue between the unconscious and the conscious. The aim is to build a bridge between the waking world and the dream world.

A good interpretation has a stimulating effect and can resolve fears associated with the dream or inner blockages. Usually the dreamer experiences a "click," and he or she recognizes connections which can help her move forward. Dreams are not simple puzzles to be solved; they are irrational, non-causal realities that are seeking to be connected to our lives. Dream interpretation, then, is a dialogue with one's own soul, and it usually takes place in a discussion with another person or in a group. A person who wants or needs to interpret his or her dreams alone can approach them with questions in order to find a connection to her personal life situation.

What questions can help us come closer to finding the meaning of our dreams? Let us imagine we have had the following dream:

> I am in my apartment. Unlike in real life, it has a wooden floor. Not only are there holes in the floor, but some of the boards are also loose. The stairs leading up to the gallery are also very rickety. Suddenly I see an animal – I only see its shadow at first. It is a hedgehog. I come closer and realize that the hedgehog is also a small human being, a baby. The little hedgehog-person wants to run away from me.

Does this dream trigger an emotion? Let us assume that the dream leaves us with a feeling of astonishment. We can then ask ourselves: in what concrete situation have I experienced a similar feeling to that in the dream? Do these feelings also play a role in my life at the moment? Our aim would be, by asking the right questions, to connect the emotions in the dream with experiences in our daily life – that is, to explain the relevance of the dream feelings for the here and now.

In addition, we might ask: which dream image makes the most vivid impression? Let us assume it was the hedgehog. We could then consider what comes to mind when we think of hedgehog – which in the dream is half hedgehog and half human being. Maybe we already know something about the nature of hedgehogs; or we can simply read about how hedgehogs live in order to get a sense of the characteristics of this dream image. The objective is to determine what the hedgehog stands for; what does it symbolize? A hedgehog is a timid, nocturnal animal. Because of its spines, we cannot stroke it or cuddle with it. Therefore, a hedgehog frequently symbolizes people who create distance from themselves through somewhat aggressive, "prickly" behavior. They often hide their sensitivity and emotionalism behind this. Now we could ask ourselves whether we also have some measure of hedgehog inside ourselves – that is, whether we sometimes react gruffly or aggressively in order to hide our vulnerability. Concrete situations in which we do not allow anyone to come near us might form the bridge to understanding this dream.

Subjective Level Interpretation

Whenever we see an aspect of a dream as a part of ourselves – as an inner, psychological facet of our personality – we can speak of dream interpretation at the so-called "subjective level." In subjective-level dream interpretation, all of the figures in a dream are understood to be personified character traits of the dreamer. The entire dream then functions as an internal drama within ourselves. Questions we ask about the dream images are then first and foremost questions about ourselves. If we want to examine the image of loose wooden floorboards or a rickety staircase at the subjective level, we must then ask ourselves about the state of our own psychic foundation. Do I feel emotionally well anchored? How stable is my self-confidence? The "footing" of our concrete lives may also be questioned: how stable is my current life situation? Could something be in danger of breaking or collapsing, causing me to stumble or founder? These sample questions can only serve as suggestions as to how the subject of a dream can be linked to one's psychological and outer reality. It is a creative process to find one's own key personal questions that can lead to the relevant themes in one's life and "hit the nail on the head."

A dream interpretation at the subjective level is a particularly appropriate approach when we dream about people or figures who are strangers to us, or whom we know only distantly. However, interpreting a dream at the subjective level can be rather uncomfortable. If an unknown thief appears in our dreams, we might need to consider whether, at some level, we might be stealing from others, or whether we have a tendency to allow ourselves to be robbed. The aim is to recognize whether we are perhaps stealing power from other people, or stealing their ideas – or whether, on the other hand, we ourselves are becoming victims of theft. An internal thief might be an indication that we frequently allow others to take advantage of us, perhaps because we are too good-natured or fearful. However, not all thieves and robbers are alike: some are brutal; others, like Robin Hood, steal from the rich and give to the poor. The Three Robbers in Tomi Ungerer's eponymous book[66] actually end their criminal career and become philanthropists, using their stolen booty to buy a castle that will provide a new home for orphaned children. Depending upon whom our dream robbers most closely resemble, the meaning of the dream can vary significantly. It makes a big difference whether we can characterize a dream thief as primarily sympathetic or purely destructive.

Not only our personal experiences and thoughts, but also stories can contribute to deciphering the meaning of dream symbols. A dream story can be compared to a story we have read or which we know from a film. What is the purpose of stories? The African author Helon Habila[67] recounted how everything became clear to him through stories. Through stories, he learned to understand the world. He listened with fascination when the older women told stories in the evenings when the extended family was gathered.

Helon Habila was probably referring to those stories which dealt with existential conflicts and crises faced by people on every continent throughout the ages. These stories are not forgotten because they preserve fascinating insights for generations to come in the form of allegories, fairy tales or myths.[68] They are concerned with something fundamental: how do people come to find themselves in difficult crisis situations, and how can they overcome them. What is necessary for a person to become an adult? What happens when we fall in love? And what is the secret of good and evil? From these stories, we learn about the typical characteristics of humankind: in Jungian terminology, we speak of *archetypes*.

Fairy tales also pick up on the fundamental, archetypical questions of humankind. Fairy tales describe typical processes in life in a symbolic form; some fairy-tale motifs can be found all over the world. C. G. Jung therefore described the language of fairy tales as the international psychological language of all humankind. Nowadays, many contemporary psychologists consider fairy tales to be obsolete, particularly because they contain too many gruesome scenes. Yet people need to be able to imagine terrible things; otherwise they will remain naïve or unprepared, since terrible things happen constantly all over the world. They do not simply disappear if we look away from them.

There are even fairy tales about the dream motif mentioned above – the hedgehog. For example, someone who dreams about a hedgehog could read the tales of "The Hare and the Hedgehog" (*"Der Hase und der Igel"*) or "Hans My Hedgehog" (*"Hans mein Igel"*) by the Brothers Grimm, to see if either of these two stories makes sense to him or her. Someone who is currently in the midst of a competitive situation in which unequal or unfair weapons are being used might be able to learn something from "The Hare and the Hedgehog." This story deals with competition and collaborative trickery or deception. In spite of his long, nimble legs and his tireless competitive spirit, the hare loses in a race against the hedgehog. However, the hedgehog does not run at all, since he recognizes from the beginning that he does not have a chance; he could never win in a fair race. Instead, he persuades his wife to play a trick: the hedgehog waits for the hare to race by at one end of the field, his wife at the other. What impresses us more: the stupidity of the hare or the clever hedgehogs who do not shy away from collective deception? Are we appalled by the hedgehog couple's trick, or can we smile at them for winning because they worked together? Or do we take the side of the hare, who tries to win honestly and with all his might? In other words, with which character do we feel a spiritual affinity? If the hare and the hedgehog are intended to represent human character traits, then we will find that a hard-working, capable person can lose in a competitive situation if he cannot imagine his opponent's cunning or recognize what measures his competitor might employ.

"Hans My Hedgehog" describes a very different problem. Since this story tells of a boy who is rejected, it is interesting for men who have perceived themselves as unwanted or unloved from childhood onwards because they are not the way their parents would like them to be. Therefore, this fairy tale is particularly relevant for young people who see themselves as troublemakers because of attention deficit hyperactivity disorder (ADHD) or aggressive behavior. A person who comes across this fairy tale in response to a dream about a hedgehog and feels emotionally affected by it can learn what is necessary in order to overcome rejection.[69]

Stories or films are helpful in understanding our own dreams if they foster our imagination with regard to a dream motif and lead us to discover a relevant theme in our own lives. Through the stories, we can learn how other people before us have overcome similar situations. Then we are not all alone with our problems.

Objective Level Interpretation

Nevertheless, every dream interpretation is merely a hypothesis, simply an attempt to read an unknown text.[70] We can never be completely sure which way of looking at a dream is the most appropriate. As we mentioned above, unknown figures and scenes in our dreams often reflect our own emotional situation. However, the situation is different when we dream about familiar places and conditions, family members, friends, colleagues or other people who are close to us. It is often correct to relate such dreams to our concrete relationships. In "objective-level" interpretation, we compare relationship patterns in dreams with our real experiences in our relationships. Differences between dream relationships and waking relationships can be particularly interesting. A student named Mara was surprised by a discrepancy of this kind when she woke up, drenched in sweat:

My boyfriend Leon is driving the car; I am the passenger. We cannot agree on our destination. Leon wants to do something different than I do, and he is not willing to change his plans. I become very angry and say: "Stop the car; I'm going to walk, no matter how long it takes."

Mara and Leon have been together for 18 months; from Mara's point of view, the relationship is going quite well. Her experiences in real life do not fit with her dream images. Therefore, she contemplates each image, one at a time, in order to discover the possible meaning of the symbols. The dream begins with the drive together in the car. This corresponds to her external reality, since as a couple, we travel through life together. In the dream, Leon is steering the car, causing Mara to ask herself who is doing the "steering" in their real life. Who makes decisions in the relationship? Who gives the directions? Do they decide in consensus, or is the decision one-sided? Mara recognizes that Leon primarily initiates decisions and she almost always agrees. She likes his ideas and suggestions, so she happily goes along with them. Through the dream, it becomes clear to her for the first time that Leon is much more active and adventurous than she is.

In reality, Mara has not had any real reason to be angry at Leon up to now. Is it possible that she did not recognize an irritation, or repressed it in order to avoid conflict? Or is she simply afraid of having a major argument over what direction to take, which might lead to their separation. Does she already sense some mild, unspoken discord that needs to be brought out in the open? Mara scrutinizes the unpleasant dream with these and similar questions in mind and attempts to better understand the pattern of her relationship. The end of the dream makes her quite uncomfortable because in reality she definitely would not want to pull away from Leon in such an angry way. But a story told by a dream does not have to become reality. The dream plays with our options; it shows us possible ways to act which we are free to reject or which we may bristle against. The dream does not force us to do anything.

The Power of the Imagination

Since Mara is not at all satisfied with the ending of her dream, she takes the last scene as a starting point for her imagination – that is, she observes where her fantasies and ideas take her. After all, a dream is not a finished product which we must accept; rather, it can be the starting point for a continuing story. Particularly in the case of nightmares which end abruptly without a conclusion and remain stuck in the middle of a perilous scene, it can make sense to enter into our own fantasy world in order to find a solution or an escape. Someone like Max, for example, who at the end of his nightmare can move neither forward nor backward because he is standing at the edge of an abyss and a monster is blocking the way back behind him, can rework the scene in his imagination.

In our imagination, we can focus all of our senses on a dream image. We can concentrate on the scene, listen to sounds, or perhaps even perceive smells or a taste on our tongues. Occasionally we can touch something or feel ourselves being touched. If we dare to venture into a fantasy world like this, we will notice that something shifts. Something will always happen to change the situation. Something which from a rational point of view may seem absurd, tiny or insignificant can be psychologically very important. When Max picks up in his imagination on the end scene of the dream we have just described, a butterfly appears beside him. Suddenly he feels joy and wishes that the butterfly would land on his hand. Max would like to simply fly away from this terrible dream situation like a butterfly: in recent months, his disturbing dreams have placed a considerable strain on his mood. He is therefore amazed that in his fantasy, he is able to feel happy and to long for something. Feelings which he could scarcely imagine anymore have become possible for him. And he knows that he has not simply "imagined" the joy; he has experienced it. The feeling of happiness was truly there. This shows how, in the space of freedom that is our imagination, we can break through seemingly unsurmountable limits and through the logic of reality.[71]

Imagination releases a person from restrictions and makes him or her into a player in a game. And in the words of Friedrich Schiller, a person is "only fully a human being when he plays."[72] Anyone who gives free rein to his imagination begins to experiment with himself, and nothing is hopelessly set in stone anymore. Everything is in the process of becoming – it may change or be transformed. A person who allows his imagination to take over is leaving a door open for surprises. Something different or new can enter his life – especially desire and hope. This will not make a nightmare disappear, but it will place other perspectives and forces alongside it. Imagination and fantasies have an effect; they are not simply "illusions."

Anyone who does not believe this or has never experienced it can discover what it is like, for example, through autogenic training. In the first two stages of this relaxation technique, the practicing person imagines his or her body becoming pleasantly heavy and calm. She then focuses her attention on her heartbeat and breathing; later on her belly and her forehead. It has been medically proven for some time that the visualizations described here have an influence on the vegetative nervous system. There are measurable changes in circulation, blood pressure and heart rate – often after only six weeks of practice. This demonstrates how quickly our minds can have an effect which is not only noticeable psychologically, but is physically measurable!

Visualizations have a suggestive effect on our autonomous nervous system. What we experience as psychologically relaxing is reflected in the body in decreasing stress parameters. Many people who practice yoga, meditation or similar techniques have the experience that fantasies, emotions and the body have a reciprocal influence on each other. Thus, one can even begin approaching and exploring a nightmare physically – for example, by dancing the individual scenes of the dream.[73] In this way, a theme or emotion from the dream can be manifested physically. Particularly when the atmosphere of a dream is difficult to comprehend, or when it is not possible to express the subject of the dream in words, the body can serve as a non-verbal bridge to understanding.

The power of our imagination to affect our emotions and our bodies – which may seem incredible to some – lets us see the healing power of dreams which was described in Antiquity in a new light. Whenever suggestions or dream images have a profound emotional effect on us, the autonomous nervous system reacts as well. This can cause symptoms to occur, but it can also make them disappear.

Consciously Shape Your Sleeping Situation

Nightmare scenes can be so terrifying, and our fear of being overcome by them again can be so great, that concentrating on the images seems out of the question. If you instinctively wish to distance yourself from the dream images, you should create that distance and wait to see what happens. Jewish tradition advises anyone who does not dare to look at his or her terrible dream images to engage in a day of fasting[74] in order to break out of the usual rhythm of his life.

A single nightmare that only disturbs us for one night without causing any lasting problems does not necessarily call for a great deal of attention. It is also certain that as long as we are still alive, we will wake up again after every nightmare. Sleep is only one half of our lives, and once we awaken, life can certainly be different than it is in a dream. It can be comforting to know that there is more than just the world of nightmares. Some people are comforted by the old piece of wisdom that reminds us that in times of fear or in an acute crisis, we should think about the birth of a child.[75] Here, one painful contraction follows another, but in the end, the child emerges. In other words, the situation does not remain terrible forever; at some point, after the mother has survived and endured the pain long enough, a change occurs.

In the case of recurring or frequently occurring nightmares, such advice can hardly provide comfort. Passively waiting or enduring does not usually bring us any further. However, if the dreamer still does not dare to look directly at the dream images

– or simply can't remember them – she can nevertheless pay more attention to her feelings in everyday life. What emotions do I experience throughout the course of the day? When do I have unpleasant or "bad" feelings? How do I cope with them? Do I seem to be dealing with them successfully, or do I feel uncertain and try to avoid my feelings? In a similar approach to the dream-affect-play therapy developed by Eckart Rüther,[76] we can write in an emotional diary every evening before going to sleep in order to once again recall the spectrum and intensity of our feelings during the day that has just ended. Given that the conscious and the unconscious are closely related to and interwoven with one another, concentrating on our own emotions during everyday waking life will not fail to have an effect on our dreams. However, we cannot predict *what* will change.

For some people, this will seem too uncertain, too complicated, or it simply takes too long. If we want to quickly take concrete steps against our fear of possible nightmares, we can also use the power of our imagination. Before falling asleep, we can search for calming visualizations. One possible inspiration could be *The Dream-Eater* (German: *Das Traumfresserchen*), a fairy tale-like story by Michael Ende about the kingdom of Schlummerland, the land of slumber.[77] Just as in real life, it is not the length of time a person sleeps that counts in Schlummerland, but the quality of sleep. In Schlummerland, the king is always the person who can sleep the best. Yet in this story, while the king is always able to get a good night's sleep, his daughter suffers from nightmares! Even though the worried king spares no effort in trying to help the little princess, traveling all the way to the end of the world, he cannot find anyone who knows of a cure for her nightmares. Finally, when the king loses his way in a dark, cold place, he meets a prickly little creature which identifies itself as the Dream-Eater. Its diet consists solely of frightening dreams; yet it does not come unless it is called. Anyone who wants to have his or her dreams gobbled up must invite the Dream-Eater for a visit.

The rhyme people use to call on the Dream-Eater resembles a prayer. If this sounds blasphemous to some, keep in mind that the Hebrew word meaning "to pray" is identical to the words for "relativize" or "engage oneself".[78] The prayer is intended to create a connection – nothing more than a bridge between our conscious mind and helpful forces of the unconscious. Michael Ende's story reminds us not only of the helpful effects of rituals and visualizations, but also of the fact that we must actively mobilize our inner helpers. It is important to make an effort and keep up hope, even when the journey seems tedious or difficult. In this process, we cannot always avoid approaching the limits of what we can tolerate.

Immersing Oneself Versus Dissociating

This could mean facing our dreamed images once again in a waking state. When a pastor once had the very unspectacular dream: "A tomato is thrown away," he assumed the role of the tomato.[79]

He experienced how the tomato became red, ripe and juicy in the sunshine. By playfully immersing himself in the central image of the dream, he was reminded of the importance of warmth and sensuality, and of how much he missed them in his current life situation – no wonder, perhaps, since in the dream the tomato was thrown away.

This kind of role play, therefore, can lead us to significant personal insights. Nevertheless, we should not overwhelm ourselves with destructive dream motifs; we should only venture back into our nightmares when we feel stable enough to do so. As soon as we are in danger of being deluged with emotions or emerging images, it is important to leave the dream scenario immediately, give ourselves a good shake or perhaps wash our hands or expose ourselves to some other physical stimulus in order to achieve some distance. Sometimes it is helpful to remove ourselves from the dream scene in our imagination and instead to send a deputy into the nightmare in order to observe the action. Assuming the position of an observer can create the distance necessary to cautiously approach once again. The aim is to explore the images and feelings that emerge when a different person is involved in the dangerous dream situation. Sometimes the deputy is able to achieve a different perspective and uncover resources or possibilities for action which we had not noticed before. Ultimately, it is important not to let ourselves become victims of the nightmare situation, but rather to become active in a form that is appropriate for us.

A somewhat different possibility for gaining access to dream action is lucid dreaming.[80] In lucid dreams, the dreaming individual is aware of the fact that he or she is dreaming. Some people are able to use this lucid consciousness to intervene in the action of the dream. In this way, a lucidly dreaming person can actively change or control an unpleasant situation. Lucid dreaming can be learned and practiced; however, in individuals who are already overly disciplined in everyday life, it can occasionally increase nightmare activity or fears. Apparently, the extension of a controlling lifestyle into the realm of sleep constitutes an imbalance that is not always beneficial. Attempts to bring the uncontrollable under control do not always seem to foster our capacity for resilience. Since resilience is defined as our ability to deal with stress and challenges, in the context of coping with nightmares, we can best increase our resilience if we increase our ability to handle frightening situations.

5. Nature as a Nightmare Motif:
Natural Forces, Dangerous Animals and Plant Life

Nature is more powerful and much older than human beings. As long as we live, we are surrounded by nature, and at the same time we are a part of it. The nature we are concerned with here is our Mother Earth. This is also the subject of Georg's nightmare:

> The earth breaks apart in front of me; the earth opens up, and I fall into a fissure. The earth is a desert.

Tumbling and Falling

In the dream, Georg is utterly alone and falling. Falling or plunging from a height is a frequent dream motif. What images does this kind of falling scene trigger in you? Does it scare you to think that it is possible to fall when you are in a high place? After all, it is a well-known platitude: the higher we are, the deeper we can fall. If you had a dream like this, it might simply remind you of that truth and prompt you to a response: under what circumstances could you lose your inner balance or have a psychological crash? What could happen if all possibilities fail? Might you fall into a depression, have a "nervous breakdown" or lose your social standing? And if you imagine the dream continuing: where might you land? Would the landing likely be hard or soft?

While some falling dreams take place in empty spaces or in nature and the dream scenario is focused on the fall itself, in other dreams the location is relevant:

> I am falling through more and more floors, from top to bottom, in my parents' house.

This dream image reminds us that the theme of falling often also touches on the question of the floor. We would not fall if we were being supported – either by a concrete, solid surface or our own stable internal foundation. As children, our parents provide us with such a foundation – both literally and concretely as well as emotionally.[81] Their love and support – as well as their morals and values – form our emotional foundation. Yet while a young person needs the support of this parental foundation, both physically and psychologically, in later phases of his or her life it can become a hindrance. Therefore, a cracked or broken parental "footing" could represent a dangerous, destabilizing break – but also a necessary one. A break is necessary when traditional support no longer takes us further. Someone who dreams, for example, that his bookcase is collapsing might ask himself whether past experiences or earlier knowledge have become outdated and whether he wants to discover more of his own – and thereby discover his own foundation.

Chasms, Barrenness and Deserts

In Georg's dream, his fall takes place in nature. Anyone who stands in front of an abyss, a ravine or a glacier crevasse is confronted with an abrupt break: a surface suddenly comes to an end and frequently breaks off sharply. A change of levels such as this occurs in nature without any reason – "out of the clear blue sky." We call this chance. Is Georg familiar with any internal chasms or drop-offs of this kind? Where might there be emotional abysses or gaps? As a manager, he is not very popular with his employees because he is a compulsive, detail-obsessed control freak who constantly wants to be informed about what is going on. He has zero tolerance for mistakes; everything has to run according to plan. He cannot let go and celebrate, relax or get carried away with anything. Georg appears to be confident and to have everything under control. Yet sometimes he seems to be "walking on thin ice." In reaction to a trivial issue, he became uncontrollably drunk and was unable to work for two days: his crash was an alcohol binge. Georg is overwhelmed by unpredictable events, as soon as he loses control of the situation. For him, a loss of control is a horror and a true abyss. His dream image unexpectedly shows him that such inner chasms are completely natural and are a part of our lives, which therefore periodically run off course.

The human journey through life from birth to death could be compared metaphorically to a hike, which begins in a location that we cannot choose for ourselves. Some people start on a level plane and hike slowly and steadily forward; others want to – or must – master high peaks, descend into valleys or fall into chasms. There are stony and difficult paths, but there are also easily passable ones. Every person follows his or her own path. One can walk straight ahead, branch off, or take detours. Some people seek adventure; others need safety, shy away from risks and walk very cautiously. Just as we cannot choose the starting point for our life's journey, neither do we usually know what places we will pass by or where our journey will end. For a safety fanatic, this is a nightmare; for an adventurer, on the other hand, it is fascinating. As a human being, to endure in encounters with an overpowering nature – to defy dangers in potentially deadly corners of the earth and to survive – these things are especially invigorating to such a person.

In his dream, Georg senses that he has fallen into the fissure, but he is still alive. What is it like there? Narrow, dark, cold – or all of these things together? How does he experience the loneliness and lack of food? Georg now finds himself in a precarious situation. Neither status nor money nor established strategies can help him here. His situation has become existential, and that is horrifying.

He is completely on his own; he will get to know himself better and more intimately than he ever has before. What will dominate

71

now: hopelessness or the will to fight? Desperation or anger? And how will he deal with this?

A person who thinks of him or herself as a fighter can visualize her own ideas and resources. What would be helpful? What is most appropriate?

A fighter might also be inspired to conquer her own "abyss" experiences by the docudrama *Touching the Void*.[82] This film tells the true story of how, in 1985, the 25-year-old mountain climber Joe Simpson fell into a glacier crevasse in the Andes. Despite great despair, a broken leg and horrendous pain, he did not give up. Since he was not able to climb up the inside of the crevasse, he rappelled down to the bottom and was actually able to find a way out. Over and over again, he motivated himself for another twenty minute period and crawled laboriously forward until, after seven days, he was found close to the base camp. Joe Simpson fought – in small steps, he tried to do what was possible for him – and he also had great deal of good luck.[83] After all, he could not have known that there was a way out of the glacier crevasse at the bottom, and he could not be sure that anyone would still be waiting at the base camp or that anyone would hear his calls for help. Nor could he have known that he would even be able to survive for so many days without food or water. Despite this uncertainty and lack of knowledge, he simply kept going and ultimately survived.

Naturally, however, experiences with an abyss – be it a real one or a psychological one – do not always come to such a good end. Sometimes we must realize that something will not end well and that we cannot rescue ourselves or the situation. What do we do then? Buddha's parable of the berry[84] teaches us what attitude is also possible in a hopeless situation: a traveler, fleeing from a tiger, comes to the edge of a cliff. In desperation, he swings himself over the edge and clings to the root of a wild grapevine. While the tiger sniffs at him from above, he looks down into the abyss and sees that another tiger is also waiting at the bottom to devour him. Only the root is keeping him safe. But to his horror, he sees that two mice, one black and one white, have begun to gnaw on the root. At that moment, the traveler sees a juicy blackberry hanging beside him. He lets go of the root with one hand in order to pluck the blackberry. It tastes delicious! Up until the last minute of our own lives – even when survival seems hopeless – nature can still hold something exquisite for us. But we must recognize it, grab hold of it and enjoy it. Even in the most extreme moment of helplessness, there can be a little room to act; we can take advantage of it or not.

As dream motifs, neither an abyss nor a desert is a homelike location for human beings. In the desert, nature is not an effusive hostess; the table is not lavishly set, and the sand and extreme temperatures endanger our lives. Yet the desert – like other regions and corners of the world that are hostile to human beings – is populated by countless animals and plants. Thus, perspective plays an important role in judging a location. A place which may be an ideal environment for certain animal or plant species may be deadly for other species as well as for human beings. The earth is always a good mother when she feeds us, keeps us warm and lets us grow in safe surroundings. As soon as she refuses us these things – for example, when she allows us to starve and die of thirst in the desert – she is an evil and deadly mother. She always has these two faces: on the one hand she gives us life; on the other she takes it away. Furthermore, she distributes her gifts very unfairly: some receive more, others somewhat less; a few get almost nothing: we sometimes call these creatures "nature's stepchildren."

In this case, the earth is a stepmother. The prefix "step-" means "bereaved" or "orphaned"; its German equivalent "stief-" means "to rob."[85] This robbery describes the contrast between a power and the lack or loss of it, for example: seeing/blind, healthy/sick, alive/dead. Such a contrast also exists in the relationship between mother and stepmother. In this sense, the stepmother is a mother who is lacking in motherliness, who deprives or robs a child from all that is maternal. This applies regardless of whether we are speaking of Mother Earth or of a human mother – because as our great, superordinate mother, the earth is a role model for every human mother. Each human mother assumes the responsibilities of our great Mother Earth at a personal level and serves more or less as her representative. Both human beings and nature are good mothers sometimes and in some places; in other times and at other places, they are stepmothers. In several European languages, the common name for a pansy *(Viola calaminaria)* is translated as "little stepmother." This name is a fitting one: the flower's five petals have been allotted differing amounts of space. The center petal has an advantage, taking up enough room for two; the two adjacent petals are normally placed; and the last two petals are forced to share the fifth space. They are stepchildren who have not been given their fair share. For the philosopher Franz Vonessen, this flower is a symbol for the vagaries of nature.[86]

The threatening character of the desert also has an impact on Raimund Gregorius, the protagonist of the novel *Night Train to Lisbon* (German: *Nachtzug nach Lissabon)* when, for a period of several weeks, he dreams about the hot, Persian desert sand which melts the lenses of his glasses and works its way into his eyes.[87] The dream motivates him not to take up a teaching position in Isfahan as planned after – in an identical, recurring nightmare scene – the desert sand robs him of his most precious possession, namely his eyesight. The dream image was a warning for him.

However the desert is not only dangerous; it is also breathtakingly beautiful. It is the desert's natural barrenness, its light and its stillness that hold a great fascination for many people to this day. Free of worldly distractions, in solitude and reduced to the bare essentials, the desert was already an ideal place for early Christian monks to concentrate on the inner world and on God. Could there also be phases in the lives of us modern human beings in which, more than ever, we require solitude with ourselves as much as we require air to breathe?[88] A person who dreams of the fascinating aspects of the desert could ask him or herself this question. Does the idea trigger something more like longing in us, or more like fear? Someone who constantly exhausts himself with external issues might see the dream image of a desert as a call to rediscover himself. Perhaps it means retreating more from day-to-day concerns, more introversion and contemplation of one's own soul. But it could also mean simplification, more concentration or more quiet: it depends upon what qualities of the desert are emphasized in the dream image and what associations find resonance within us.

Weather, Storms and Volcanoes

The sun warms the most powerful, but also the weakest – healthy people as well as sick ones.

When it shines, it is not intended for us personally, but we feel personally spoken to. Thus, the weather is a popular topic of conversation nearly every day, all over the world. Sometimes it makes us happy; often it gives us reason to complain – in part, perhaps, because we do not have any influence over it; we must constantly accept it. At the same time, we have different personal preferences: some people love the summer; it can never be hot enough for them. Others prefer the colors and temperatures of autumn. For many people, spring – bursting with new life – is the most beautiful season. However, even the atmosphere of winter – with life in a state of repose, with its cold and sparse light – is loved by some.

As people, we almost always have an opinion about the weather. However, the weather and nature have no opinion about us. The weather and nature are simply there; they are a given. We can adjust ourselves to them to the extent that we go outside or inside and we dress appropriately. But we can also escape the weather by traveling to another place where we can expect weather conditions to be better. The situation is similar with our moods, feelings and emotions – they represent our internal weather. They, too, appear without being asked, and we have to tolerate them. Sometimes we indulge our feelings, but if we find them burdensome or disturbing, we may sometimes run away from them – that is, attempt to suppress them.

Dreams that have to do with weather conditions, therefore, could also symbolize an emotional state – whether it is our own or something in our surroundings. And in accordance with our personal preferences and ways of dealing with external tempera-tures, our attitudes toward moods and emotions also differ.

In a dream, Felix is at the mercy of extremely stormy weather:

> I am sitting directly beside the ocean, slightly above it; I am eating in a tavern. I spot a tornado approaching from the ocean. I jump up and want to warn other people. It is too late. The tornado snatches me up and pulls me into the air with a violent force.

Felix remembers that when he was young, a cigarette manu-facturer was allowed to advertise using the slogan: "*Wer wird denn gleich in die Luft gehen? Greife lieber zu HB.*" ("Who is ready to fly off the handle (literally: 'go up in the air')? Better reach for an HB.") Smoking was thought to mitigate intense emotions or kept them from occurring at all; it supposedly kept people from becoming "ungrounded" by their emotions. Today, we still use weather-related vocabulary to describe certain types of behavior: we may flare up, bluster, be tempestuous or like a whirlwind. With their tremendous, elemental forces such as rage, fury or panic, our emotional storms can do a great deal of damage. Some people can feel how such emotions erupt from the depths of their bellies and are finally discharged. We can compare this to an erupting volcano, spewing its hot lava out from the center of the earth. Ancient myths are also familiar with the connection between a volcanic eruption and an outpouring of rage. They tell of dragons that live inside volcanoes. When they become angry and fight with one another, the volcano spits out fire; but as soon as the dragons make peace, the volcano is extinguished. These things that happen in the bowels of the earth can be a metaphor for the processes which occur inside our bodies and our souls.

Dreams about volcanoes or volcanic eruptions could therefore point to a possible eruption of our emotions. In what contexts are emotions problematic – and when are they helpful or perhaps even necessary? That would be our next question. Some people have a tendency to gather up their anger or rage; that is, they sup-press their annoyance or resentments for a long time and appear outwardly peaceful. When there is no longer any room left inside for new anger that emerges, everything which has been stored up suddenly explodes and vents itself in one enormous, violent stroke. At best, this can take the form of a very vehement reaction; however, it can also result in rampage. It is therefore important not to underestimate an emotion. Someone, for example, who dreams of having a jovial picnic at the edge of a volcano and then notices with amusement that it is starting to spout smoke and fire, is probably misjudging the gravity of the situation and overestimating him or herself.[89] It is not without reason that we are warned against dancing on a volcano.

If a volcanic eruption or a violent storm appears in a dream to symbolize our emotions, then it becomes clear that we ourselves are not identical to our emotions; rather an emotion is a naturally-occurring inner force which can take hold of us.[90] Phrases like, "He was overcome with rage" remind us that anger initially has control over us, and not the other way around. People who fly off the handle easily – perhaps too easily – might wish to examine whether it is appropriate to constantly live out their affect, or whether, perhaps, they even secretly enjoy intimidating those around them. Perhaps, however, they simply provoke "a storm in a teacup" rather too often.

Yet sometimes we need the exuberant energy that comes from this kind of volcanic rage, because it provides us with the passionate fire and superhuman strength through which we can free ourselves from rigid external or internal prisons. In particular, someone who likes to keep him or herself under control might discover, through a dream about volcanoes or thunderstorms, that this very tempestuousness is now available to him and may be put to use. Here, the glowing lava might symbolize a wild, archaic sexuality with excessive sensual experiences that is now coming to the surface. The lava is the expression of elementary forces and instincts. Here, rage, passion and dread are closely connected, as we are reminded in Erich Fried's collection of poems, *Es ist was es ist. Liebesgedichte – Angstgedichte – Zorngedichte (English: It Is What It Is: Love Poems – Anxiety Poems – Anger Poems).* [91] [92]

The Animal Within Us

The statement, "I'm turning into an animal" implies that reason, education, morality or societal conventions are being rejected and that raw animal instinct is gaining the upper hand. When people dream that they are animals, they might ask themselves whether it could imply this kind of disinhibition. Everything that we attribute to our brains may be lost. The dreamer may also ask him or herself how it feels to be transformed into this animal. What ideas are triggered if we move or live like the animal? What are the specific characteristics of the dream animal? Is it a solitary creature or a herd animal? Do I feel some kind of connection or closeness with the animal, or does it repulse me?

It makes a big difference whether one can see and fly like an eagle, or is the King of the Beasts like a lion – or whether one is transformed into a pig. Eagles and lions are noble, regal animals, so it is usually easier to identify with them – unless one is afraid of flying or does not like to be the center of attention. Scarcely anyone wishes to be a pig, a cockroach or a rat. This not only has to do with the nature of these animals, but also with the fact that these animals symbolize something. We attribute something particular to certain animals. Thus, we speak of the cunning of a snake, a clever fox, or the king of the air. In proverbs, myths and songs, we learn something about the symbolic nature of animals. And in turn, we ascribe these animal symbols to individual human beings. When a popular song from the 1990s says, "You have to be a pig in this world," we understand the symbolic meaning; and someone who responds to this text might wonder whether, in a sense, he or she has such a pig inside of her.

The Chinese also believe that we are spiritually connected to certain animals. In their view, every twelve years, a similar type of person is born, who can be described with one of twelve animal symbols. The corresponding animal in the horoscope symbolizes character traits which are intrinsic and essential to that person. Yet something which is plausible in one cultural group may meet with astonishment or rejection in another. For example, since cows are considered dumb by most Europeans, but are sacred in India, it makes a difference whether a European or an Indian person is dreaming about being a cow.

Whenever an animal is at the center of a nightmare it is worthwhile to keep its nature and cultural symbolism in mind. If we understand why a certain animal poses a threat or why it is despised in a certain culture, we can consider whether this particular aspect is relevant to our own current life situation. If these considerations do not lead us any further, we can also look for the positive aspects of the animal symbol. A symbol always contains light and dark characteristics, yet we have a tendency at first to consider only one side. When someone fights like a lion, this can be positive and powerful but also brutal and therefore negative. And in addition to many negative aspects, we also associate a snake with the valuable power of regeneration – among other things, because it is able to shed its skin. Even the natural characteristics of an animal that we fear are not exclusively negative. Perhaps it is an expert in the art of living under difficult conditions, or it has extraordinary abilities which may lie dormant within us as hidden resources and could be helpful in our own lives.

In general, it is rather unusual to dream of being an animal oneself; much more frequently, we dream of meeting animals in our dreams, as in the case of a 50-year-old woman named Iris:

> Several sharks are swimming around in the large pool of an indoor swimming complex. Many people are standing around; most of them are my fellow teachers. I have some large pieces of meat that I want to feed to the sharks. Two of my colleagues want to grab the meat away from me and throw it into the water themselves. I refuse to let go, but the meat falls into the water – and if we are not careful, we will fall in as well.

What does the image of a shark conjure up? Do you think first of the danger to human beings? Or are you attracted by the fascination of dealing with a life-threatening situation? A pearl diver, a marine biologist and a tourist would probably all have different feelings with regard to sharks. Many people are afraid of sharks, but occasionally they are part of our lives or our professions. There is probably no species of animal that certain people do not find fascinating. Some people study their habits; others fight to preserve the species; still others are interested in them for medical or pharmaceutical purposes. Depending upon how much we have to do with a certain animal and how close it is to us, a dream can have different interpretations.

Iris is afraid of sharks because they can kill human beings. In reality, she would never willingly approach an open pool filled with sharks, let alone feed them. She is shocked by her careless behavior in her dream; it is not like her at all. Only the struggle with her two fellow teachers seems quite familiar to her. Recently, Iris has felt increasingly demoralized by the many conflicts occurring between her colleagues. People are constantly arguing about who should take responsibility for an upcoming project and how the tasks should be divided. She often feels disregarded and has the impression that her opinion doesn't really count. She doesn't feel capable of standing up for herself.

If the dream reflects concrete interactions among the staff, then Iris is not as helpless as she feels in real life. In the dream, she is not the victim of the situation; she participates actively in the dispute. Did she perhaps not want to acknowledge how energetically she actually participates in the arguments? In the dream, the conflict contains two levels of imagery: the human level and the animal level. Iris and her colleagues are outside the pool; below them in the water, the sharks are waiting to be fed. All of the participants seem to be interested in providing the carnivores with food. There is even a competition to see who gets to feed the dangerous animals first. Is it possible that the subliminal atmosphere among the staff currently resembles a competing tank of sharks? Are certain colleagues feeding the cold-blooded, predatory aspect that lurks inside every person and thereby destroying a good working atmosphere? If this dangerous game continues – the dream implies – the participants might land in the shark pool and be seriously injured. Yet the dream also shows that neither Iris nor any of her colleagues has become a shark. They have not yet been completely consumed by a killer or predatory instinct. They are free to feed the sharks or not. A de-escalation of the conflict still appears possible.

Thus, a subconscious, animalistic side may be involved in human conflicts. Depending upon what species of animal is keeping the conflict alive in our dream, a different quality will unconsciously be activated in us. So, for example, we speak of "fighting cocks" that attack one another, or "dog-eat-dog capitalism," in which people fight like animals for supremacy and power.

The Snake

Sharks are wild animals which we cannot tame. A shark in a dream is a confrontation with an uncontrollable emotional force. We encounter such autonomous instinctual forces in dreams about snakes. They can fill us with fear, as demonstrated by Brigitte's dream, which occurred in the night after her first encounter with a man she had just met:

> I am in my apartment. The door to the terrace is open. A fat snake is coiled up in the garden. I scream and immediately close the door, my hands shaking. The snake slithers forward, rears up and looks at me angrily through the glass. It flickers its tongue and wants to come in.

What ideas are triggered by the image of the snake? What would it be like to touch a snake or to have one in your house? The snake is a significant symbol in almost every culture. In Christian culture, it is seen as a great tempter or seducer: it incites Eve to eat the forbidden fruit and disobey God's taboo. The consequences of their action are well known: the couple was banished from Paradise.[94]

The Biblical snake represents human beings' desire for knowledge of good and evil, which led to a dramatic change of location: they were forced to leave the Garden of Eden. In some parts of Indonesia, a snake in the house is believed to herald an imminent relocation. Similarly, the appearance of a snake in a dream can signal a decisive change. It frequently refers to a disruption or a shattering experience which could set our lives in motion – analogous to Adam and Eve's expulsion from Paradise. The snake wants to tempt us toward knowledge, but also toward desire and sexuality.

Brigitte experiences the dream about the snake following her first meeting with a man she met through the Internet. There was a spark of attraction at first sight, and after an hour together in a café, Brigitte felt as if she had already known this man for a long time. They agreed to see each other again on the following weekend. However, on the way home she began to have doubts: is he really seriously interested in her? After all, he lives far away. Will he disappoint her too? In her dream, she meets not her potential partner, but a snake. The snake wants to come into her house, but she refuses it. Is it sexuality that Brigitte fears? Or does she fear the changes that a relationship could bring? Does she have a tendency to want to remain alone in order to protect herself? According to the dream, the relationship problem lies first of all with her. This idea surprises her, because she longs for a relationship and would like to live with someone as a couple. But sometimes the same things we wish for are those which we also unconsciously fear. In an intimate relationship we are vulnerable, and as soon as we enter into one, we are also dependent. By this I mean that we mean something to one another, we are "attached to each other," and the other person is not indifferent to us. This is completely natural, but nowadays, our independence is very important to us as well. We also want to be free, so we try over and over to strike a balance between these two conflicting needs. Great unconscious fear of intimacy and closeness can cause us, like Brigitte, to close ourselves off – to shut the door and not let anyone enter, so to speak. This causes us to miss out on some experiences, but at the same time, we save ourselves from possible disappointment.

In the dream, the snake – and therefore, everything that it symbolizes – wants something different than the dreamer. Instinct and the dreamer are in disagreement, because while the animal seeks closeness, the dreamer wants distance. Yet when an animal seeks contact with someone in a dream, the dreamer does not always succeed in keeping it at a distance. Sometimes an animal succeeds in touching us gently, not letting us go, biting us or killing us. In the process, the animals may approach us shyly, roughly or aggressively.

In the following dream, Maria is unable to prevent a snake from coming much too close to her:

> In a swimming pool in front of me, snakes are jumping around wildly on the surface of the water. Suddenly a snake jumps at me and sucks itself tightly onto my head. In my dream, I have a vivid, physical feeling of the snake; I want to shake it off behind me, but I cannot get rid of it. A voice says: "You have to shake it off to the front!"

For Maria, having the snake attached to her head is a horrifying experience. Whatever this snake may symbolize or intend to do, Maria absolutely wants to get rid of it. If she were able to shake the snake off behind her back, she would no longer be able to see it. And as soon as we no longer see something or do not have to look at it, we can sometimes have the illusion that it no longer exists. When we want to put something behind our own backs, this might be a metaphor for a psychological wish to repress something. All human beings repress things throughout their lives; this is a natural, and frequently a healthy psychological mechanism. Repression is fundamentally neither uncommon nor harmful. But repression can become destructive if it leads to psychological or physical symptoms.

In her dream, Maria seems to want to repress something. In reality, Maria has the feeling that something is not right with her. For several months, she has been brooding and ruminating too much. The same thoughts pester and torment her over and over. It is as if they are stuck inside her head – similarly to the snake. Now she wants to treat her repeated, circular thinking with psychotherapeutic medication. The dream occurred on the night before her visit to a doctor. Could it be taking a position with regard to her wish for medication? In the dream, a voice advises her to change her strategy: the snake should not be thrown behind her, as Maria intended; rather, she should throw it in front of her. In that way, the snake would fall into her line of vision and could not continue to have a hidden effect on her from behind.

However, looking at something means the opposite of repressing it: it means confronting it and becoming conscious of it. Medication cannot do this. It is a mental and emotional process within a person. Nevertheless, even if the dream speaks in favor of this mental/emotional process and conscious confrontation, this does not mean it forbids Maria from taking psychiatric medication. It is up to her to decide whether she needs the medication in order to ease her suffering. Perhaps the medication will provide her with the inner foundation she needs in order to consciously deal with her worries. Perhaps, however, the dream also lets her see that she can count on her own ability to undertake a conscious confrontation. With this resource, she would be able to do without medication.

Horses and Donkeys

Of course, a touch from an animal has a very different quality than a bite, which we usually experience as painful and threatening:

I go for a walk. There are other people walking as well. Suddenly, a spirited stallion comes running toward us. He runs directly up to me and bites hard into my hand. I scream with pain. Several other people scream and run away in a panic. The stallion will not let go of my hand, no matter how hard I try to shake him off.

Ute describes how beautiful and wild the stallion is in her dream. Why did this spirited animal cause her such pain? Unlike a snake or a shark, a horse is a mammal and is much more closely related to human beings than a reptile or a fish, which cannot be tamed. Like a cat or a dog, a horse can also form an emotional bond with human beings and become a companion for them.

Today, many girls want to learn to ride around the beginning of puberty. Once they become interested in boys and sexuality, however, horses are often no longer important. Here, an important aspect of the horse's ancient symbolic meaning could be shining through: horses symbolize physical urges, sexuality and potency. When a young girl learns to ride, she comes into contact with these animalistic aspects and experiences what it is like when two bodies discover a mutual, harmonious motion. This can also unconsciously bring about a change in her fears of sexuality.

Whereas horses, like all animals, have a natural sexual instinct, this is not true for human beings. In other words: wild animals are not unnatural. Only human beings can be unnatural, since they can resist their natural physical needs such as hunger, sexuality and sleep and control them in abnormal ways. This means, first of all, that natural physical urges – and sexuality in particular – are not so simple for human beings to live out as they are for animals; they are much more complicated and more easily irritated.[95] Thus, an encounter with a horse can create a bridge to our own sexuality and natural instincts.

Ute also enjoyed riding as an adolescent, but she has not had an opportunity to do so for many years. Her work as a consultant brings her little enjoyment, and her contact with her co-workers is quite superficial. Privately, she lives quite reclusively alone with her cat and spends her free time studying philosophy and religion. It has been some years since her last relationship with a man, and sexuality no longer interests her. Yet in her dream, she is bitten by the lively stallion. Biting does not always have to be destructive; it can also be erotic. If the bite from the horse is painful, it may also point to the connection between desire and pain. The painful bite from the horse might be the means that the director of her dream resorts to in order for her to finally realize what is urgently needed in her life: physicality and sexuality. In fact, when something follows us or attacks us in a dream, it may simply want to live with us and no longer be shut out.

A young musician also had this experience during a performance tour. Between rehearsals, she often went riding together with a very attractive colleague. Since on principle, she is faithful to her husband, rumors to the contrary had made her very angry. An affair is out of the question for her.

She has the following dream:

> A voice says to me: "You have an enormous amount of strength." I ask in astonishment: "What kind of strength is that?" The voice answers: "The strength with a horse's hoof."

Upon awakening, the dreamer recognizes immediately that the horse's hoof belongs to the devil. The thing that is demonizing her – namely, forbidden eroticism and sexuality – is also stirring within her. This Christian devil is a descendent of the ancient god Pan, to whom moral commandments meant nothing; he was only concerned with spontaneous desire.

As a rule, we cannot constantly repress or neglect our spontaneous, natural cravings if we want to remain physically and emotionally healthy, and it is amazing how often our dreams remind us of this fact. They warn us not to forget about nature. This can take place in the form of a pursuit scenario, but it can also be very direct, as in in Elke's case. This freelance architect in her late forties very seldom remembers her dreams, much less her nightmares – until one night she wakes up shivering and in a sweat:

> I am in an apartment; it is my home. A friend asks, "What are you doing with the donkey? It is starving! Have you forgotten about it?" I say, "My God, I really did forget about it. It hasn't had anything to eat for over a month, and it has nearly starved to death." The donkey can hardly walk; it looks at me reproachfully, suffering in silence.

Elke notices that the apartment in her dream, unlike her real apartment, is neither comfortable nor orderly. The friend who asks her the friendly question is a stranger; the shaggy, emaciated and neglected donkey is crouching in the corner. In the dream, Elke knows that the silently suffering donkey will just manage to survive, but she is horrified and irritated at her own behavior. In reality, she would never let an animal go hungry. Instinctively, she asks herself if she has unconsciously neglected something important in recent weeks. Certainly not her work: for months now she has been snowed under with orders and sits in her office even on weekends. However, because of her professional stress, she has hardly paid any attention to her own physical needs. She sleeps too little, eats irregularly, and no longer finds time to exercise. For a few weeks now, she has noticed a chronic, gnawing pain in her stomach. The discomfort is a nuisance; she even gets angry about it sometimes.

As beasts of burden, horses and donkeys also carry people. The dream image of a horse or a donkey can remind us that our bodies carry our egos – our souls and our minds – similarly to a donkey: patiently and usually in silence. On days when we feel healthy, our bodies operate almost discreetly in the background; we can practically forget about them or pay little attention to them. They do not interfere with our usual obligations, pleasures and efforts. When we sometimes expect a lot – or even too much – from our bodies, we assume that they will not notice; they will tolerate it or forget about it quickly. However, we are sheltered within a knowing body, as this poem by Robert Gernhardt[96] reminds us:

Noch einmal: Mein Körper

Once again: My body

Mein Körper rät mir:
Ruh dich aus!
Ich sage: Mach' ich,
altes Haus!

My body advises me:
Take a rest!
I say: I will,
old house!

Denk' aber: Ach der
sieht's ja nicht!
Und schreibe heimlich
dies Gedicht.

But I think: Oh,
it can't even see this!
And I secretly
write this poem.

Da sagt mein Körper:
Na, na, na!
Mein guter Freund,
was tun wir da?

Then my body says:
Now, now, now!
My dear friend,
what are we doing here?

Ach gar nichts! sag' ich	Oh, nothing! I say,
aufgeschreckt,	surprised,
und denk': Wie hat er	and think: How did it
das entdeckt?	find out?
Die Frage scheint recht	The question seems
schlicht zu sein,	very simple,
doch ihre Schlichtheit	but its simplicity
ist nur Schein.	is an illusion
Sie läßt mir seither	Since then, it won't
keine Ruh:	leave me alone:
Wie weiß mein *Körper*	How does *my* body
was ich *tu?*	know what *I* am doing?

Not only do our bodies know what is going on with us, but they also speak to us, whether through physical symptoms or in a nightmare experience. These are our bodies' options for gaining our attention. And rather like a donkey, our bodies can be quite stubborn, repeatedly reminding us in their own language that they work autonomously and reliably, but that they also need our care and attention. Nowadays, however, we hardly actually have any time to attend to the needs of our bodies if we want to keep increasing our productivity and efficiency. Therefore, some people would be happy if they were able to control their bodies still better, or even to overcome them. But without the foundation of our bodies, our mental and spiritual lives as we know them would also die.

A horse in a dream as a symbol for the body and the instinctual, animal world solidified a diagnosis approximately 100 years ago, when modern methods for neurological examination were not yet available. In this case, doctors were in disagreement as to whether a young woman was suffering from the early stages of a fatal muscular atrophy or from a psychological disorder. When C. G. Jung[97] examined the young woman, she told him about a dream in which a horse was careening around inside her apartment; finally, it jumped out of a window onto the street and lay there, smashed to pieces. These dream images gave Jung the assurance that the woman was suffering from a severe organic illness in which the body would destroy itself.

Human Beings as Enemies of Nature

It is not only a nightmare when a person is threatened by the powers of nature, but also the other way around: when a human being destroys nature. This is true both in reality and in dreams. Just as animals can attack us, human beings are also capable of brutality toward animals, as in the example of Richard, who awoke from the following dream with a racing heart:

> A rat is sitting on my terrace. At first I want to chase it away, but then I hit it on the head with a metal shovel. I am afraid that the rat is only knocked unconscious, so I position the shovel at the back of its neck in order to cut off its head. The rat is badly injured; its head is hanging off, but it runs away as blood spurts out.

Richard suffers from feelings of inferiority. With his short stature, his low-level position at work and his shy manner, he feels unattractive to women. After the dream, he lies awake for a long time and worries about his cold-blooded brutality, until he suddenly realizes that the rat is a part of himself which he wishes to destroy. Although he dislikes rats, he is uncertain whether it was right to strike this one dead.

As plunderers of food reserves and carriers of disease, rats are unpopular with many people. "You rat!" is therefore used occasionally as an insult in our part of the world, describing an underhanded, devious person. And when "the rats leave the sinking ship," we know that either the perpetrators of a debacle are trying to shirk responsibility for it, or sycophants and profiteers are turning their back on the situation so as not to be pulled down with it. Nevertheless, as omnivores, these rodents are extremely adaptable and resilient. This tenacity may be incorporated into the German expressions *Leseratte* (literally, "reading rat" – an avid reader, equivalent to the English "bookworm") or *Wasserratte* ("water rat," meaning a good or enthusiastic swimmer). The enthusiasm and intensity with which some people dedicate themselves to reading or to the element of water is frequently a positive character trait. These types of positive connotations predominate in the symbolic significance of rats in Asia. There, the rat is seen as an animal which brings happiness and prosperity.

So what does this mean for Richard? He does not particularly like himself, and would like to be a very different man. This rat which he wishes to kill may symbolize the parts of himself that he rejects. However, if he were to kill it, he would also destroy part of his own vitality, and that is problematic.

The killing of an animal in a dream is often a destructive act, but under certain circumstances it can be a necessary one. Someone who kills an animal in a dream should consider what relationship he or she has to his own animal instincts and how he deals with his own body. To put it more simply: on the one hand, there is the extreme of an overly cerebral life, in which the body is seen as a burdensome evil. On the other hand, there are people who unconsciously follow only their physical instincts without reflection and severely neglect their mental and spiritual development. Based on these two extremes, in mythological terms, the overly cerebral person needs to better care for and feed the animal aspect within him or herself, while in the other case, the animal must be conquered and sacrificed. In the mythological language of dreams and fairy tales, the latter is sometimes depicted as the act of killing. Therefore, people who need to reconnect with their instincts and their own natures in order to remain healthy should not kill the animal under any circumstances. This would be a threat to their existence. Others, in whom the animal within them takes up too much space, will need to kill it in order to become more human. These two positions demonstrate that we can either exaggerate or understate the instinctual side of ourselves and that it is necessary for us to find a good balance.

Dogs and Cats

Dogs and cats are popular house pets. However, they are not particularly fond of each other; therefore we sometimes speak of two people who do not get along well as "fighting like cats and dogs." This saying presumes, then, that we may have some traits within us which resemble those of cats or dogs. When Martin dreamed about a dog, however, he related it not to his character, but to a decision-making situation:

> I am taking a walk with my wife and some friends; we are walking alongside a fence. We are in a good mood. Many flowers are blooming in the meadows; it is early summer and pleasantly warm. Suddenly, I am continuing to walk alone, and shortly afterward I come to the end of the fence. A large dog is waiting there. It stands in front of me and bares its teeth. I am terribly afraid.

The end of the dream depicts a confrontation between Martin and a strange dog. The two of them stand face to face, without the separation of a fence. What could this encounter mean?

Dogs are sensitive and very loyal friends to human beings. Someone who trains a dog can experience how reliably and obediently it follows rules. A dog can learn to protect a house, to locate drugs or other substances with its keen sense of smell, or to safely guide blind people. On the other hand, every dog owner also experiences how much the dog needs him or her: the dog must be fed and taken for regular walks. Thus, loyalty, commitment, and mutual guidance are core themes between human beings and dogs, and they can also be relevant for the interpretation of dreams.

In Martin's dream, an additional motif appears to be important. The dog appears at a border – namely, at the exact point where the fence comes to an end and Martin is standing alone without his wife or his friends. This reminds us that in Greek mythology, dogs are associated with Asclepius, the god of healing, and with the area of transition between life and death. In this context, the dog symbolizes a place in which we could go in one of two opposing directions: on the one hand, there is the path to good health and back into life. On the other side is the realm of the dead, guarded over by a dog.

Martin really does stand at such a crossroads, because now, in his early thirties, he is suffering from advanced cancer. His doctors are uncertain whether he will live much longer. Interestingly, the dream is very precise in depicting the season of early summer; this season "fits" very well with the young age of the dreamer; we occasionally speak of the age of retirement as the "autumn of our lives." The dream picks up on this ominous threshold situation without indicating any prognosis. The direction in which Martin's life journey will continue is left open.

Cats can call other subjects to mind, as we clearly see in Lena's dream:

> In a large, light, empty room with a wooden floor, a man sits feeding a yellow, tiger-striped cat. I know the man; he has been a good friend of mine for many years. He feeds the cat slowly from his hand. Then I hear soft, gentle cracking sounds. I see that my friend has both his hands on the cat's muzzle and is breaking its jawbones. He slowly breaks all the bones in the cat's body. The cat is quiet; it doesn't cry out or defend itself.

Unlike a dog, a cat cannot be trained. As a freedom-loving creature, it is only prepared to adjust or submit to human beings to a certain extent. It has nothing like the dependent relationship that exists between human beings and dogs. Its attachment behavior has a different quality: after rambling through its territory, it returns to its human companion only when it needs something. Its first and foremost obligation and loyalty is to itself. Whenever it is hungry or wants to be stroked, it tries to gain our attention in order to get its wish. Yet it is selective in its appreciation, and it communicates well-being by purring. This penchant for pleasure and desire for a self-determined existence may have contributed to the fact that, beginning in the Middle Ages, cats were demonized and vilified as the companions of witches. At that time, women who were denounced as witches were primarily those who

– similar to cats – attempted to maintain some degree of self-will, independence and enjoyment of life, rather than conforming to patriarchal structures.

In Lena's dream, her friend kills a cat in a barbaric manner. Could the cat possibly symbolize her own spirit animal – or that of her friend – which is in danger? Whose inner cat could be threatened with destruction? Her friend has many exciting plans for his retirement, but he somehow seems unable to make good use of the freedom he has gained. It seems to overwhelm him, and in recent months he has seemed increasingly passive and joyless. Interestingly, in the dream, it is not her friend but a cat who is the victim. If Lena's dream represents her perception of her friend's emotional reality, then he would be the offender who is killing a piece of his own soul. He is destroying an instinctive power which knows how to lead a self-determined life and enjoy it. The dream might be encouraging her friend to connect with his cat-like nature and once again shape his life in an active and self-determined manner.[98]

Plants in Nightmares

Expressions such as "She is a delicate little flower..." or "What a shrinking violet! ..." are already indications that from a symbolic point of view, we can also be similar in nature to plants.

At the physical level, the metabolism process within our cells, the cellular assimilation and utilization of oxygen as well as the vegetative nervous system correspond to the biological life processes of plants. Analogous to plant growth, inorganic material gives rise to somatic, chemical reactions in the human body. We do not consciously perceive these physiological processes – just as it is not possible to tell whether a plant can experience joy or pain. Only external signs such as dry leaves or infestation with pests can show us that a plant is not well.

Plants grow remarkably well in the presence of people with "green thumbs," even if those people do not necessarily feel that they are especially good at caring for plants. We cannot know whether or not a loving hand encourages plants to flourish – we can only assume so. A plant cannot give us any direct information on this point. Plant images in dreams, however, can speak metaphorically and make references to psychological or physical correlations. For example, someone who dreams about a withered branch might ask him or herself whether something alive inside of her is in danger of drying out or dying. And what thoughts are provoked by the idea of a lack of water, without which nothing can live? Someone to whom plants are unimportant or who perhaps even has an aversion to plants might pay little attention to a dream image like this one, whereas plant lovers would be likely to prick up their ears. Nightmares, on the other hand, leave almost no one unaffected:

> I am in a beautiful setting. Suddenly, a severe thunderstorm begins. I see three birch trees; one of them is struck by lightning.

Monika is awakened by the force of the lightning bolt. The middle tree of the three is completely broken and charred. The fire has destroyed it; it is dead.

Sayings like, "He's as solid as an oak," "The apple doesn't fall far from the tree," or "A tree is known by its fruit" compare human life with a tree. In earlier times, the so-called "sympathy tree" which was planted at the birth of a child was thought to be a *doppelgänger* of that child and closely linked to his or her fate. If this tree takes root well, the individual will also put down emotional and worldly roots and can withstand stormy periods in life. On the other hand, we speak of people who have lost their external or spiritual home as being "uprooted." And like those of a tree, human roots are not directly visible. What ultimately supports us, and the actual state of our primordial source is not obvious; rather it is a secret – perhaps a divine one.

In the nightmare experienced by the Biblical king Nebuchadnezzar, the network of roots remains undamaged when a heavenly guardian comes down to fell a tree, which reaches all the way up to the sky.[99] It is explained to the king that he himself is this tree and

94

that it is God's decision that his reign will be taken away from him. However, the intact root system guarantees that Nebuchadnezzar will be able to retain his power if he does not continue to place himself above God. Twelve months later, when he has once again forgotten that even he cannot achieve anything without divine support, he is indeed overthrown and becomes temporarily insane. He learns the lesson that human trees do not actually "grow all the way up to heaven."

The vertical growth of a tree can therefore represent human aspirations for spiritual maturity, higher ambitions, or even claims to power that extend as far as rivalry with God. A person who imagines him or herself to be unassailable in his potency, sense of power and influence is sometimes reminded of this type of hubris through the dream image of a felled tree.

However, according to the Jungian analyst Marie-Louise von Franz, the destruction of vegetal life in a dream can also be an indication of physical death. In numerous dreams about plants, she detected clues to the end of physical life. Drastic images such as these – a favorite tree in the garden is cut down; a field of wheat is trampled by wild boars; or a fire burns a forest to the ground – may herald physical death.[100]

Thus, 60-year-old Monika, who is ill with cancer, is certain that the image of the tree destroyed by lightning is a reference to her death. However, the dream says nothing about a possible time when her death will occur; only that it might come suddenly, "like a bolt from heaven." We imagine death as a natural occurrence, no matter how bitter it may be for us human beings.

Not only plants, but plant pests may also be at the center of a nightmare:

> I am doing a big clean-up. My sister Amelie is sleeping in a bed. I am about to clean near the head of this bed when I notice a swarm of small creatures at her neck. They are living scale insects that are building a nest. I am horrified.

A colony of scale insects does what it always does – namely, suck the life out of its host. Here, the victim is not a normal one (a plant), but the sister of the dreamer. And since she is asleep, she cannot notice what is happening to her. The dreamer has a very good relationship with Amelie, and she tells her about the nightmare. Amelie feels somewhat tired, but she does not feel drained or sapped of life. She cannot imagine that the dream refers to her until three months later, she is diagnosed with cancer.

This dream might actually be a premonition of Amelie's physical illness. After all, it takes an average of three to seven years before a malignant tumor becomes large enough to be detected. Before this time, we cannot perceive the cancer cells: metaphorically speaking, we are sleeping. And during this beginning stage we often have no worrying symptoms of any sort. The dream image of the scale insects could be a clue that the cells of Amelie's body were weakened – comparable to a plant which is exposed to a massive infestation of these insects. Metaphorically, the disease of cancer is sometimes compared with small creeping animals which attack and devour our organs. These images are not merely popular folklore. A dictionary definition of cancer goes as follows: « Everything that slowly and silently gnaws, hollows out, spoils or pulls out.»

6. Human Beings as a Nightmare Motif: Aggressive People and Vulnerable People

From the very beginning, our real lives are threatened in many different ways. However, what seems to traumatize us more than anything else is violence and suffering inflicted on us by other human beings. Therefore, it is hardly any wonder that nightmares dealing with human aggression or brutality can cause us extreme fear. For example, a 40-year-old woman named Petra had the following dream:

> I am lying in bed. Suddenly, a strange man, dressed in black, bends over me and tries to strangle me. He already has his hands on me when a second man immediately attacks him and kills him violently with a heavy blow.

The dreamer is in mortal danger. Yet without hesitation, an unknown helper strikes down her attacker. Both the attack and the rescue occur at rapid speed. Petra awakens, agitated and drenched in sweat. At the same time, she feels relieved to have escaped with her life in the dream scenario. Yet she is also disturbed by the deliberate killing that has saved her. Why is she dreaming about such violent scenarios?

When we dream about our own death or danger of death, the subject is rarely our physical death; it usually refers to a death within our own lives – a radical separation. When, for example, we say "That person is dead to me," we mean that we want nothing more to do with a certain individual in the future and that our relationship is at an end. A radical change of heart is also a kind of death, because an attitude or opinion has died within us and made room for a different point of view. In this respect, a death in a dream may also signal a creative change, because space is being made for something new. At different levels, within the course of our lives, something or other is dying almost constantly: over and over, we have to accept that something has ceased to exist – or we consciously and deliberately bring something to an end. Metaphorically speaking, in the former case, we have to accept a death; in the latter, we actively bring it about.

Both physical death and symbolic death occur in our lives in many different forms. Death can come about gently, gradually and painlessly, but it can also be violent. Petra's dream depicts the latter: its subject is murder. And where there is a killing, there is a perpetrator and a victim.

Aggressors and Victims

A dream involving perpetrators and victims leads to questions such as these: Are there situations in which I have been a victim, or could I become a victim? What means do I usually use to defend myself when I am threatened? Under what circumstances would I be capable of killing?

In reality, we are normally terribly afraid of becoming victims. Paradoxically, however, the experience of being a victim is easier for most of us to tolerate than that of being a perpetrator. Perceiving oneself as a victim seems socially acceptable; by contrast, experiencing oneself as an aggressor is usually frowned upon or even shameful. How is this possible?

The fact is that we encounter perpetrators and victims not only in the concrete, external world, but also as potential effective forces within ourselves. After all, from early childhood onward, we all gather experience as "victims" and "aggressors." As little children, we frequently experience ourselves as small, helpless and at the mercy of others: for example, when a stronger person – usually an adult – requires us to be obedient, adaptable or well behaved. As vulnerable children, we slip into the victim role again and again, particularly when we experience the more powerful adults as aggressors, as people who suppress us or hold us in check – that is, as perpetrators.

All of these aggressor-victim experiences are stored in our memories in their entirety and filed away in our complexes according to subject. Each complex includes our actions as adults as well as our experiences as children. We can speak of two different poles of a complex: the adult pole and the child pole – that is, the aggressor pole and the victim pole. Thus a complex corresponds directly to a perpetrator-victim constellation.[101] It may seem exaggerated or harsh to apply the term "aggressor" to the adult pole of a complex. Yet in the original sense of the word, "aggression" means to go to a place, to approach, begin or take something on. First and foremost, therefore, aggression has to do with movement and intention. Such action can take place in a peaceful or in a destructive manner. In the same way, the experience of powerlessness on the part of the child or victim pole can vary between beneficial dependency and destructive oppression.

Since both poles of a complex – both sides of an aggressor-victim complex – are therefore always present in our unconscious, we are all fundamentally capable of functioning as a perpetrator or becoming a victim, depending upon the pole with which we identify ourselves.

Interestingly enough, in real life, many people have an easier time identifying with the child pole of the complex – that is, with the victim side – than they do with the adult pole, which is an aggressor or perpetrator. Perhaps this victim pole, which dominated our experience in the first years of our lives, is simply more familiar to us than the aggressor pole. Or perhaps we also expect more attention and care from others in the victim pole. Our Christian heritage could also play a role, since a victim is more likely to be considered a good person who deserves something or is owed something, while an aggressor is usually considered to be a bad person who incurs blame for his or her actions. However, sometimes it is appropriate to become an aggressor oneself. There are situations in which we can only free ourselves from paralysis, helplessness and passivity – that is, from the child position – and find freedom to maneuver if we defend ourselves courageously and aggressively.

Petra's dream shows us how helpful – indeed, how necessary for survival – aggressive action can be. On the inner stage of her dreams, two aggressive actors complete for her in a dramatic triangle. One of them wants to kill her; the other can save her. What might the two men represent? In the course of telling her dream, Petra intuitively realizes that the two strangers represent two opposing points of view. Just a few days ago, when she was confronted with a diagnosis of cancer, she decided against conventional medical treatment without hesitation. The idea of subjecting herself to the torture of chemotherapy or radiation treatment was unbearable to her. She wanted be treated exclusively through natural healing methods, since she was convinced that cancer patients could also be healed through more gentle therapy. Yet the dream caused Petra to think twice. Was her initial idea of rejecting conventional medicine really reasonable, or was she putting her life at risk? Would she have to radically dismiss the idea of using only alternative medicine in order to survive?

The dream images are violent, but the dream ends well for Petra. In this or similar dreams, it is important to identify what is helpful in a dangerous situation. Nevertheless, saving power is not always where one expects it to be; this could be one possible point of this dream. For some people, it might seem unusual or even unacceptable that help can or must arrive in a violent form.[102]

The Dream Ego

Petra's dream speaks of potentially destructive tendencies or aspects within the dreamer. Nevertheless, the dreamer herself

– the so-called dream ego – is not violent. The situation is different in Sarah's dream:

> With a sharp knife, I cut pieces of flesh out of the right side of my hip and eat them greedily. It does not bleed. Then I cut off my left hand, and then my left forearm. I am about to put some of this flesh in my mouth when I suddenly feel disgusted. I do not want to look at the cut-off flesh, and I throw it into the garbage can without looking.

Sarah's dream is a one-person scenario. Her dream ego acts brutally, beginning to mutilate herself and eat pieces of her own flesh, but also to throw them away. The aggression originates with the Dream Ego and is directed at herself. Here, the aggressor and the victim are identical.

In reality, Sarah has been a vegetarian for many years. Strangely enough, however, a few days before having this dream, she suddenly had the desire to eat a steak, even though an appetite for meat had become completely foreign to her. Had it not been for the dream, she would not have paid any further attention to this brief moment of craving. However, the dream tells not of a craving that she thought was long gone, but of an absolute voracity for flesh – the flesh of her own body.

Since separating from her partner, Sarah lives alone and is completely absorbed in her work as a senior physician at a university hospital. She is esteemed for her expertise, her conscientiousness and her commitment. She is not lacking for recognition. Her life seems to function; most things work in a smooth and orderly manner. Nothing is very exciting, and she is actually quite content. Only this dream has disturbed her, since it is a stark contradiction to her external reality, of which greed and revulsion are not a part. Thus, it could be compensating for something.

What could this thing be? Spontaneously, Sarah thinks of an advertising slogan that says "Meat is a slice of vitality." In fact, meat or flesh really is a symbol of liveliness and vitality. But here we are referring not so much to meat on a plate but to the flesh of our bodies. Someone who, for example, "has no meat on his/her bones" – meaning he or she is emaciated – becomes physically weak and feeble. Without flesh, only the skeleton remains, and then we are inevitably dead. Without flesh, we cannot experience sensuality or feelings. Mardis Gras or Carnival is also concerned with meat and the desire for flesh. The word "carne vale" can be translated as "flesh, fare thee well!" The body is allowed to enjoy itself during Carnival. It can pursue its desires until Ash Wednesday; then it bids goodbye to carnal desires with a "farewell!" In this ancient ritual, a time of carnality is followed by a time of doing without.

Thus, when Sarah dreams about a ravenous desire for flesh, she might be reminded of her own forgotten physical desires and thereby also of her lust for life. In recent years, her passion and lust for life, as well as her desire for sex, have disappeared. This simply happened gradually and without her noticing. However, when something very important or vital to life slips away or is repressed, our hunger for it can become greater and greater and we may become psychologically blocked. Yet the dams cannot remain in place forever; at some point they break. When our unfulfilled needs and desires wash over us, we might sometimes become ravenous. This greed signals a bottled-up, unbridled, accumulated demand. Thus, when we downplay one aspect of our lives too much, it can return in an exaggerated form as compensation.

Nowadays, many people are induced to go to extremes as a result of their complex to perform. Experiencing our own capacity to perform, constantly challenging ourselves and expanding our horizons all feel very good and make us attractive to others. Yet this way of living is not stimulating and healthy for everyone over the long term. Some people "devour themselves" in this way: they let themselves "be consumed" by their work. Thus, they do damage to their own vitality when they place their highest priority on productivity and give short shrift to their desires and enjoyment of life.

Like every other complex, a performance complex also has two poles: at the adult pole, we identify ourselves through expertise, productivity and discipline. At the child pole are counterweights such as idleness, "chilling out," daydreaming, and also spontaneity. Here, we resist having everything planned out and structured; we have no desire for efficiency; we simply want to be. If this child pole is not given any space at all, not only can our bodies and spirits become exhausted, but our lives can become stale or even meaningless. We often experience a life that functions too mechanically or too monotonously as worthless. Yet if, metaphorically speaking, we "devour ourselves," we should not throw ourselves, but rather our lifestyle onto the garbage heap. It is not a lust for life that is our problem; it is the life we have not lived.

Only these drastic dream images were able to make Sarah realize that she was living her life as a "well-functioning, high-performance machine." Since the dream depicts her as both aggressor and victim, it is primarily her own responsibility to pay attention in the future to whether she is merely functioning or whether she is also living. This kind of attentiveness to one's own vitality is important not only for Sarah, but as a prophylaxis against burnout syndrome. If, for example, we want to avoid falling into the role of a victim, we should not betray our feelings. In some cases, we may let ourselves be convinced to do something even though we sense that something is not quite right about it. We burden ourselves with something because we dare ourselves to, because other people encourage us, or because we see it as a career opportunity. It is then easy to make the sacrifice of an uncomfortable feeling in favor of rational considerations.

Naturally, it is not appropriate to shy away from responsibility every time one has a "bad" feeling. But if we dare to confront these "bad" feelings instead of immediately silencing them, we may be able to avoid becoming the victims of our own expectations or excessive demands early on. It is important to face up to any inner conflict between a bad feeling and positive enticements – that is, to take both sides into account.

The Child in Dreams

In the dreams of Petra and Sarah, their respective dream egos were under threat. The situation is different in Markus's dream: his 12-year-old daughter is in danger:

> I have to watch as a strange man slowly pierces my daughter in the belly with a knife with the aim of killing her. I want to scream, but no sound comes out of me.

In reality, Markus is the father of a grown son as well as the daughter who is being attacked in his dream. Could his daughter actually be in some kind of danger, or does the dream address a danger to Markus's inner child – his inner, emotional daughter?

From time immemorial, parents have had ideas about their own children. They may wish for their child to have specific talents, interests, or simply a better life. Such parental hopes or expectations can challenge a child and encourage the development of his or her talents, but they can also be dangerous. In fact, nothing can alienate a child more from himself than his parents' efforts to project themselves into their child, if they do not keep in mind that every child is a new, individual creature who sometimes may scarcely resemble them – or in extreme cases, may seem alarmingly unfamiliar to them.[103] But what can it mean for the parents, when their child is so radically different from what they know – and perhaps value – in themselves? For some parents, this is a shock. The different nature does not fit into their world view, and it disturbs and unsettles them.

When a child is so different, it can happen that parents unconsciously wish to destroy this undesirable part of their child – symbolically speaking, they want to kill it. Let us imagine a somewhat stereotypical family whose children have been skilled craftspeople for many generations. What might happen if I child who was "all thumbs" were born into this family? Perhaps the parents would be disappointed, but perhaps they might also be angry or simply perplexed because they cannot understand how anyone could be so unskilled at manual tasks. Such a child can easily become the "black sheep" of the family. The features that are considered "black" are ultimately decided within the family; however, it also depends upon the values of the society in which that family lives.

Markus, too, has quite specific ideas with regard to his children. From his point of view, his older son is progressing well, but he has some concerns about his daughter. What will become of her? While all the other members of the family have easily made their way through school and university and are successful in their respective professions, his daughter has no interest in school. She does not like to study; instead, she spends all of her free time at the neighbors' farm. Markus does not like this; however, up to now, neither incentives nor punishments have increased her motivation for schoolwork. Yet Markus is shaken by the dream. Might a part of him – namely, the strange man – unconsciously wish to destroy his daughter? Might the part of him which becomes visible in real life when he aggressively puts his daughter down cause her severe emotional damage and threaten her psychological vitality? She is not happy in school; she is happy with animals and at the stable. Markus cannot understand this; nevertheless, he wishes his daughter happiness, even if she finds it in different places than he does.

Markus bristles at the dream images. He does not want his daughter to suffer any harm. He can only really preserve her vitality if he stops trying to force his own way of life onto her and gives her more room to develop in her own unique way. Perhaps he can even become curious about her different interests and understand this as an expansion of his own perspective on life. Metaphorically speaking, this process can allow a black sheep to become a colorful personality in the family.

In Markus's case, a child became the black sheep because she did not live up to his expectations. However, the same thing can happen when a child is too good – that is, when he or she has interests or talents that could extend beyond the family's traditions. If a family cuts such a child off from his potential and squelches his development, in metaphorical terms, they can also psychologically kill that child.

Markus observed his dream at the object level: that is, he directed his attention to his relationship with his daughter. This was the correct approach for him. However, this does not rule out the possibility that the same dream also contains a signal at the subject level that refers him to his own endangered inner child – his endangered inner daughter. The child motif in a dream often points toward something new – toward future potential and development. For example, someone who dreams about an unknown three-year-old child might consider whether there is something new which entered his or her life approximately three years ago: a new love, a new job, a new apartment or something else. This could be the bridge from the dream child to the person's real life.

Thus, the age of the dream child can indicate the length of time that something new has been living and working within us. If this approach does not lead you any further, you can look back at your personal life history to when you were the age of the dream child. What was your attitude toward life at that time? Did you have an experience during that phase of your life which could be relevant to your current life situation? What memories and images come back to you from that time? When a 42-year-old man named Simon dreams about a young boy who makes him feel afraid, he instinctively thinks back to his own youth:

> I am standing in front of a black boy, approximately 14 or 15 years old; he is sad, profoundly sad. He is crying. The reason for his sadness is a loss. I feel very threatened by this boy. Suddenly, white patches appear on his body which then spread out over large areas of his skin.

Simon is a cautious person. It is very important to him to keep his life on an orderly, secure course. Privately and professionally, his living conditions are stable, and he has no worries. Intense feelings and emotions play no role in his life at the present time. Through the dream, however, he is confronted with a phase in his life in which his feelings were on a roller-coaster. He recalls the sad moments from his life at that time – for example, how he secretly cried when he was unhappily in love.

Does Simon's youthful sadness still frighten him today? Or is he in danger of suffering a loss which could reopen old wounds? What images does he associate with black skin and the color black? What kind of relationship does he have with dark-skinned people? Depending upon his personal experiences or attitudes toward dark-skinned people, his own skin color, as well as his preference for or aversion to the color black, the core meaning of this dream could be quite different.

In addition to our subjective associations, the culture context of our dream images can assist us in interpretation. For example, in our Western culture, loss, sadness and the color black all go together. To this day, widowed people or mourners at a funeral usually wear black clothing as a way of communicating their situation to the outside world. Up until a few decades ago, one year of mourning was considered appropriate for bereaved persons; after that, they were no longer expected to dress in black. From that point in time onward, it was permissible for the survivors to turn toward life again, and widows and widowers were allowed to remarry. In this way, mourning was not only an individual experience; it was also embedded in a societal code of behavior and a temporal order.

Simon does not dream of a sad boy dressed in black, but of a boy with black skin. Unlike a person's clothing, however, we cannot simply take off or change our own skin. Therefore, in Simon's psychological world, the black boy might symbolize an old experience of mourning which has lived unconsciously within him for more than twenty years – until just recently. But Simon sees that the blackness is becoming lighter. The boy's skin does not remain completely black; rather, it is becoming white in more and more places. A change is taking place, even though the dream does not give an indication of the background situation. Simon had this dream at a time when he was undergoing psychotherapy, which he had begun because of a conflict at his workplace. Up to now, the experiences of his youth have not been a subject. He interprets the dream as a suggestion that in his examination of himself, he should also be concerned with repressed fears of loss and feelings

107

of grief. Confronting these things instead of looking away can help make loss and grief into something that is not exclusively shrouded in darkness. In addition, dark areas of our souls can become lighter as a kind of side effect, if we deal intensively with a situation which, at first glance, has nothing to do with our early experiences.

A child in a dream does not always lead us to a turning point in our childhood or youth. A dream child can also represent the child that lives within us: something small, inconspicuous, perhaps not completely comprehensible that wants to find further expression. Or it could refer to something childish that affects us stemming from our complexes or from our past. We can come closer to explaining the symbol of this inner child if we consider what it means to be a child in a general sense. The younger a child is, the more dependent it is, and the more it must rely on its parents' care and attention. But this does not always remain the case: as he or she grows older, a healthy child will continuously gain independence, strength and autonomy. Thus, when we dream about a child, this aspect of providing care can be important. In what instances could we be needed around the clock, analogous to caring for a real infant? In what situation do we require a great deal of energy and time, are able to sleep very little and are fully absorbed in something new? A new relationship, a new job or a move to a new home could place this kind of demand on us – but in some cases, so might a new emotional development. Yet similarly to a real child, the thing which claims so much of our attention can, through our efforts, become stronger and more stable.

However, being a child also implies a certain way of living, with which adults have often lost contact. The playful, effortless manner in which children ask even serious questions; their openness and their capacity for love, joy and pleasure are no longer something natural or taken for granted when we become adults. In light of this enviable capacity for fantasy, creativity and spontaneity on the part of many children, the psychiatrist Helmut Barz[104] wondered what it is in people's upbringing which – from the starting point of such promising childish assets – can produce the miserable adults that some of us become. Thus, a child in a dream may raise the question of whether this childish way of being has become buried and whether it might want to be brought back to life.

Particularly at times when we feel dissatisfied or stagnated, or when we don't know how to go on and old formulas no longer work for us, we need something completely different, symbolically speaking: an inner child as a new possibility. Similarly to a real baby, an inner baby can introduce some disruption into our lives and turn our accustomed habits on their heads. An inner child can have an amazing effect, similar to that of real children who visit elderly people in a retirement home. Often, the old people open up and blossom when children come to visit. Their childish energy is transmitted to others, and it activates a long-buried joy of life or seemingly forgotten resources.[105] This dynamic is not fundamentally dependent upon age; therefore, an inner child has the potential at any point in our lives to enliven our spirits and to break up seemingly unalterable or rigid patterns – if we allow it to do so.

However, a child in a dream does not necessarily symbolize new creative potential: in some cases it may also represent childish behavior that is no longer appropriate for our age. Perhaps there is an immature, dependent or underdeveloped part of us which we need to overcome. Someone, for example, who dreams about a truculent child might ask him or herself whether she also sometimes behaves in a stubborn manner and whether or not this is actually still helpful for her. If someone says that he or she does not feel nearly as old on the inside as his biological age it would therefore be important to differentiate: has this person retained a basic, childlike quality and the ability to develop himself further – or has he, in fact, come to a psychological standstill?

Paternal Authority

Wherever there is a child, there must be parents. And as long as we live, our ability to feel or react like a child is oriented toward people whom we experience as maternal or paternal. Not only can our biological father "feed" our father complex, but other figures such as a grandfather, teacher, our "father" state or government, or a public authority can do so as well. These experiences are internal images which we repeatedly project unconsciously onto various people; that is, we transfer them to other people or situations. Projection also means that to a certain degree, we unconsciously expect that our old, familiar images will be reinforced. They may be addressed in dreams, even if neither a child nor a father appears there. This is evident in Katharina's dream:

> I am in my bedroom; I am lying in bed and want to go to sleep. Suddenly a strange man is standing there: a tall conductor wearing a uniform; he is coming to check my ticket. I am terribly startled; I want to get my ticket and then realize that I don't have one. The man writes something down. I am afraid.

We constantly experience checks and inspections, be they from conductors, customs officials, police or tax authorities. What images do such inspections tend to trigger in you? Do you feel confident because you have followed the rules and therefore have nothing to fear? Do you feel uncomfortable even though you have been honest? How does it feel for you if you are caught breaking a rule? Or does it annoy you that someone is allowed to control you at all? Perhaps you have a tendency to be dishonest in certain situations, or you secretly enjoy outsmarting institutions and their representatives. Depending upon a person's attitude toward authority figures, this dream could have very different meanings. Someone who regularly rides on buses and trains without paying and is proud of not getting caught might ask him or herself whether she is not, in fact, secretly afraid or troubled by a guilty conscience. Perhaps the act of fare evasion or some other dishonest behavior is unconsciously not quite as nonchalant as it may seem in reality.

However, someone who – like the dreamer – never dodges fares in real life – would wonder why a conductor has invaded her bedroom. After all, a bedroom is a very intimate, non-public space in which a conductor certainly does not belong. Normally he works in a train, checking to see whether passengers have paid for their tickets, and he is allowed to sanction fare evaders.

Katharina makes an association between her dream and George Orwell's novel *1984*, which tells the story of a surveillance state. In order to eradicate intimacy, individuality and personal opinions, the people in *1984* are under observation constantly and everywhere, similarly to the television show *Big Brother*. In a similar way, Katharina's dream bedroom is no longer private; an authority figure is able to enter and inspect it. Furthermore, the act of checking tickets gives the impression that Katharina requires permission – that she must pay for the right to go to sleep, to rest or simply to be there.

In the patriarchal Judeo-Christian tradition that has existed for over 3000 years, it is the fathers who decide what behavior is allowed and what is not.[106] One of the very first official acts carried out by the Biblical father-God in the creation story is the enactment of a prohibition – which, however, Eve and Adam do not obey. As we know, they are punished for their disobedience. But anyone who enacts laws requires the power to enforce them. Without power, authority is not possible. All those who are expected to obey the rules must be weaker and less influential than the lawmakers.

Children experience this kind of power imbalance when their own father, or perhaps a teacher, insists that rules be followed. From a very early age, children have the experience that father figures are powerful enough to enforce their orders. This can provide children with a reliable framework and a good basis for orienting themselves; however, it can also frighten them or cause them to become angry or rebellious. Throughout our lives, such experiences with father and authority figures unconsciously influence our expectations in personal relationships, our relationship to authority and even our dealings with ourselves – even though the previously natural imbalance of powers is no longer the same.

Just a few days after having the dream, Katharina is angry with herself because she reacted like a little girl and allowed herself to be intimidated by the conductor. She is not at all happy about her subservient behavior, which is actually alien to her. In her youth, she was the only one of her siblings who dared to rebel against their father. She still has strong memories of her feelings of triumph when she was able to win in a power struggle and hold her own against her father. Does she perhaps have a blind spot here? Katharina notices that in the dream, she failed to throw the conductor out of her room. She should have defended her private sphere. Yet the fear of being punished if she were not able to show a ticket had intimidated her to such an extent that she did not even notice her embarrassment. In fact, the question of whether we are at fault or not is sometimes not simply a question of guilt, but also of shame. This connection between blameworthiness and shame is already evident in the Bible. After Adam and Eve ate from the tree of knowledge, they recognized that they were naked and covered themselves with fig leaves. Thus, knowledge of good and evil is necessary in order for us to feel guilty or ashamed at all. This makes guilt and shame the privilege of human beings: they do not exist in nature.

The word "shame" means "to cover" – and correspondingly, feelings of shame stimulate in us the need to hide our bodies as well as our most intimate thoughts and feelings from the sight of other people. However, we also want to hide when we do something illegal, such as evading fares. After all, as long as we remain undiscovered, no one can punish us. Here we are concerned with guilt and feelings of guilt – with questions of conscience. If we are caught, however, it can also happen that we not only feel guilty, but we also feel exposed. Whenever too much of us becomes visible, we experience shame. And because of this shame, we are not so much afraid of being punished as we are afraid of failing in front of other people – which is why we want to "sink into the earth" out of embarrassment. We want to annihilate and obliterate ourselves. Shame threatens us at an existential level, and unlike guilt, we cannot "pay it off" or compensate for it. We can only avoid being shamed by having an intimate space whose door no one can open without being invited. We alone decide who may enter here and who may not. Our bodies are also such a space which no one can approach too closely without permission and whose boundaries need to be respected by others in order that we can maintain our dignity and not be shamed.

If Katharina interprets the conductor at the subjective level as a representation of an inner father figure, she might ask herself whether she sometimes lets herself feel ashamed in situations of conflict with authority without being aware of it. Perhaps she reveals too much of herself or allows herself to be judged and criticized even if it is not appropriate. Katharina is certainly not unique as far as the subject of authority and shame is concerned. Participants in television shows such as *American Idol* allow themselves to be judged onstage by "experts," and sometimes pay little attention to their boundaries of shame in the process.

When, in dreams, we are judged by experts, are required to repeat a final exam or are involved in an argument with authorities, our father complex and the accompanying childish feelings of powerlessness may be relevant subjects. Yet is it even appropriate that men and fathers establish the rules? Should women and mothers not have any power to establish and enforce rules? Symbolically speaking, there are feminine and masculine categories of law and power. *Delivering Hope* (German: *Die Hebamme – Auf Leben und Tod*), a film based on real events, illustrates how these two qualitatively different laws can come into conflict with one another. The film takes place in 1815 and tells the story of the midwife Rosa Kölbl. She traces several cases of infectious childbed fever to the holy water which she is required to administer vaginally to pregnant women if the life of the unborn child is in danger. The church insists on this emergency baptism ritual in order to prevent the baby from dying a heathen. When Rosa defies this regulation during a difficult birth in order to spare the expectant mother from infection, the church sees this act as a grave transgression. Rosa is no longer allowed to practice her profession.

Which laws apply in the case of Rosa and the church? Rosa is on the side of Mother Earth, who places all living things in an established order according to the laws of nature. These include the course of illnesses and disease. Someone who, like Rosa, knows that bacteria entering the vagina of a woman giving birth can give rise to childbed fever is acting in the service of life if she bears this in mind. A person, on the other hand, who gives priority to emergency baptism considers him or herself primarily bound by an overriding spiritual principle – the supposed law of God – and wants to prevent this from being broken.[107] Both sets of rules apply to men and women alike – the laws of nature as well as cultural laws. But might it be the case that because of our respective biological genders, we have more affinity for one category or the other? What do paternal rules and patriarchal power structures mean for men, and what do they mean for women?

Masculine Identity

Not only our father's power, but also his powerlessness can be threatening to us: a 30-year old man named Klaus had the following dream:

> I am lying down and relaxing on the sofa. My father leans on me and becomes heavier and heavier, but at the same time he becomes steadily weaker. I hardly have enough strength to carry him; he becomes like a child. Suddenly he pushes into me; he begins to fuse together with me. I begin to panic.

Facing a weak father, one is in a superior position; there is no longer any danger of being patronized or held back. Someone who is longing for generational change – who perhaps hopes that his father will finally retire from business – could breathe a sigh of relief here. Yet we know how difficult it is for powerful men to step down from their positions and make room for their younger successors. When, for example, training requirements become more and more demanding, this does not necessarily have to do with concerns about the quality of the trainees' education; rather, it also secures the position of the parents' generation. As long as more and more demands are imposed on pupils and students, they are ensured of remaining in the role of children. Only qualifying examinations allow them to finally take the place of the previous generation. Thus, power and authority are awarded cyclically. Initially, the strong father dominates the weaker child. As the child steadily gains strength, the father slowly becomes weaker, and at some point he can be stripped of his power.

Sometimes, this natural progression is reversed. If, for example, a father is an alcoholic, or has failed professionally, the child might feel that he or she is superior. Yet here, these feelings of superiority arise chronologically too early and they can often trigger feelings of shame. The child is ashamed of the father because he is not capable of assuming a father's customary role.

If, for example, a little boy says, "When I grow up, I'm going to be a journalist like my dad," then he is identifying himself with his father's professional role. But this kind of fantasy is only possible if he can admire his father as a great and strong father. And with the statement, "When I grow up, I'm going to marry my mommy," the son is daring to compete with his father and replace him as a husband. For a healthy little boy, these types of fantasies are common and helpful. The father acts as a role model, demonstrating how to become a man and how one can live as a man. A mother cannot do this. However, if his father is too weak, a boy cannot emulate him. He cannot admire him; instead, he will be ashamed and in some cases may even disdain or hate him.

In his dream, Klaus does not experience a relationship conflict with his father; instead, he becomes one with him. What ideas does a "fusion" scenario like this invoke? What does it mean to completely lose one's distance from another person? What does it mean to merge oneself with a beloved, admired father – and what would it mean if the father were sadistic and brutal?

On the whole, we resemble our parents physically and emotionally to a greater or lesser degree; however, we are never identical to them. There is always a difference between us; and in this dream, that difference is nullified. In particular, people who definitely do not wish to become like their own fathers seem to unconsciously have a special spiritual connection to them. And someone who, like Klaus, has hated his father since his early childhood, can sometimes have the illusion that antipathy is the best protection against closeness. Yet hate binds us together – sometimes more than love or affection – at the very least when we can no longer think of anything but revenge.

Klaus refuses to utter the word "father," even though his own father is long deceased. Instead, he speaks of his progenitor. As a youth, he swore to himself that he would never touch a single drop of alcohol so that he would never, under any circumstances, sink to such a low point as his alcoholic father. He freed himself from the desolate conditions of his family through great discipline and ambition, and he now has a successful position in the real estate business. To this day, memories of his past with his constantly intoxicated father evoke only feelings of disgust and revulsion. It was exactly these feelings which were present in his "fusion" dream and upon awakening. Now in his early fifties, Klaus had not imagined that his past could catch up with him again in this way. The distance from his father, which he had struggled to maintain throughout his life, has been broken down in this dream.

Klaus might ask himself whether he has now reached an age at which his father's weaknesses are an issue for him again. Does he no longer feel completely fit in his body and mind? Is his own productivity decreasing? Is he occasionally impotent? Even if he does not have a problem with alcohol, has he developed other addictive tendencies which he has denied up to now? If he does discover weaknesses of his own, there is a danger that he will begin to despise himself in the same way that he used to despise his father. Someone who experiences weakness as something very threatening and always has a hard time tolerating it may be in danger, as he or she grows older, of considering his life to be worthless. However, there is also a danger that he will quickly begin to despise any family members, friends or colleagues if they display any form of weakness.

Here, then, becoming one with one's own father means losing or sacrificing one's unique identity. We are not living our own lives, but preserving the paternal tradition – both psychologically

116

and concretely. However, it makes a difference whether a man identifies with his father and strictly continues the latter's tradition, or whether a woman tries to do the same thing.

Feminine Identity

What could it mean when a woman becomes a father figure in a dream – and changes her gender in the process, as in the case of Christine?

She had the following dream:

> There is a strange, eccentric old man: thin, bearded, dressed in gray. All around him, masses of gold are piling up at rapid speed to form a cave. Now the cave is finished. A voice says that the old man could line the cave with liquid gold. I am this old man. Now only the entrance to the cave remains open. The old man/I want to close the cave completely. The voice does too. It makes a suggestion, and lets two tree trunks grow together to block off the entrance to the cave. Now the old man – that is, I – must scoop up gold with a shovel and slap it into the space between the tree trunks. The tree trunks are completely brown; otherwise, everything else sparkles with gold. The old man – that is, I – cannot do it. The walls of gold I build in the empty spaces collapse over and over. The old man/I keep repeating, completely obsessively: "I must be more careful, I must be more careful!" Only if he/I can manage to completely close up the cave will it remain standing.
>
> The scene changes. The old man/I stand there, still dressed in gray rags. The golden cave has disappeared; everything is gone. He/I keep shoveling. The bizarre tree trunks are still there. Instead of gold, the old man is now flinging lumps of dirt at them. He repeats over and over, like a crazy person, completely obsessed and delirious: "I must be more careful, I must be more careful." He throws more and more dirt between the tree trunks. The wall will not stay up. Now the entire landscape

is barren and desolate, brownish-gray. There are only bare trees standing around; there is nothing that is green or alive. The gold is gone as well. "I must be more careful, I must be more careful, I must be more careful."

During the entire dream, Christine lost her female identity. Instead, her dream ego turned into a "shabby," "ragged" old man. Unconsciously, Christine is possessed by this father figure. What is it like for a woman to become her father? Is it enticing, repellent, or neither?

Biologically, we enter the world as either men or women – although every embryo initially contains the possibility of developing into either gender. In order to support unambiguous development, the structures for the respective opposite gender die away in the course of pregnancy; however, small physical remnants remain.[108] Our psychological identity is normally female or male in accordance with our physical gender. Yet the ancient image of Yin and Yang demonstrates how, in every man and every woman, a small physical and psychological portion of the other gender still exists: the teardrop-shaped, white Yang – the masculine principle – surrounds a black center point; and conversely, the black Yin – the feminine principle contains a white center point.

Psychologically, however, the principle of the opposite gender may become so dominant that the original, natural balance is inverted. This is the case when a woman is completely dominated by her inner male characteristics – the so-called animus[109] – or a man by his female characteristics, the so-called anima. But is this a problem? Shouldn't every woman and every man be allowed to live the way she or he wants to?

In any case, Christine experiences in her dream what it can be like when the patriarchal aspect is dominant within a woman. In the dream, a golden cave forms around Christine all by itself. This is wonderful, since caves can provide protection and security, and as long as they have an opening, a person can retreat inside but is also able to go back out into the world. And who would not be pleased about the gold – which we value more than ever since the recent financial crisis? Thus, if a woman identifies herself with the psychologically masculine patriarchal world and is interested in ideas, intellect and science, a valuable spiritual space can be created.

But then the situation goes to an extreme: the old man wants to completely close off the cave. This will transform the cave into a golden cage in which the dreamer would be imprisoned and forced to live without any relationships. Thus, if a woman becomes masculine, this does not necessarily lead her to freedom; it can also become a prison. And ever since the days of the ancient King Midas, for whom everything he touched turned into gold, we know that gold has not only positive aspects. The benevolence of the gods also had its pitfalls: his food became inedible. An excess of riches can also become a curse.

In the end, the old man fails in his building project, and Christine is spared from the prison – as valuable and glittering as it may have been. Yet in the dream, the story ends in a desolate, nightmarish alternative. Mother Earth – the feminine Nature – is barren and lifeless.

The dilemma illustrated in the dream is frequently relevant for women, who reject many things related to their femininity and find the world of their fathers and of men in general significantly more attractive. Nowadays, women can live much more similarly to men than they could in earlier times: not only because this has become more socially acceptable, but also because they have become more independent from the natural processes of the female body – for example, through contraception. Even their tasks as mothers can now be delegated to a large extent. These and other factors have given women opportunities which were never there before; however they have also limited their freedom in new ways – for example, through overflowing appointment calendars.

One example of what identification with a patriarchal psyche can mean for a woman in extreme cases is anorexia. Femininity is experienced as threatening. And when a woman starves herself, her feminine attributes, such as breasts, rounded hips and menstruation actually do disappear. Her body becomes masculinized, and she is no longer capable of becoming pregnant. This could be symbolized by a barren, infertile landscape. Yet in the process of fighting against her female body, an anorexic woman often develops her intellectual abilities. However, this intellect is only destructive for a woman when the intellectual/patriarchal world becomes her inner refuge and misleads her into destroying the needs of her body and her femininity. Intellectual development allows a woman to gain psychological riches (in the dream it was gold), but her female identity must not be sacrificed at the same time. The dream warns against making such a sacrifice and engaging in a battle between body and mind – or between nature and culture – which, without any reconciliation, can end in desolation. Only when the body and soul can allow each other room to exist and can live side by side will life be fertile and productive.

In Christine's dream, there is a central motif which repeats itself: being careful. What ideas do we associate with the theme of being careful? How important is caution in real life? In what situations is Christine careful, and when is she not careful? In what situations does she take risks – and when does she not? Does she consider herself to be a courageous woman who can also act with daring and resolve? Or does she know herself as a hesitant, accommodating or even inhibited woman? She can examine the motif with the help of such questions. However, in addition to its personal aspects, the dream may also contain a general warning against extremism. Caution is always necessary when a woman unconsciously identifies completely with her inner masculinity, but also when a man identifies with his inner femininity.

In this regard, the dream also has to do with the life models which women in society may adopt. Whereas in the 1960s, it was still taken for granted that a mother would stay at home to care for her children, nowadays this model is not only frowned upon, but it is even practically condemned. It seems that even today we are not free of prejudices, but rather that in the spirit of our age, we favor a small number of possible life structures while vehemently rejecting others. This is unfortunate. If, for example, we would allow the Greek goddesses of the Olympic age to serve as our role models, we would be less rigid and could enjoy a much larger range of possibilities in our lives. Then there would be women who, like Athena and Artemis, unapologetically choose not to have children; like the ever-jealous Hera, arguing with her Zeus; like Demeter who are completely fulfilled through their motherhood; and like the sensuous Aphrodite who have multiple affairs. Such a rich variety of feminine existence would be a true emancipation and would enable those who choose certain life models that are currently rejected by our society to finally live without a guilty conscience. In fact, a number of so-called neurotic misadjustments are not actually the result of adverse psychological development; they are simply models for life which our current zeitgeist rejects.

Motherliness

Anyone who reads the stories of the Greek gods and heroes will also dispense with the preconception that women are generally nurturing, weak or masochistic. Nevertheless, 43-year-old Klaus is appalled at the brutality of his mother in a dream:

I am in my apartment when my mother knocks down the entrance door, frame and all, with two blows of a hammer.

The subject of the dream is intrusion. To this extent, it has some basic similarities to rape dreams and dreams about the violation of boundaries.

What might a mother be like in reality who uses such violent means to gain entry in a dream? Some mothers interfere constantly in their children's affairs, or they always need to have the last word. Someone who finds this behavior irritating, but tolerates it more or less through clenched teeth, could have a dream like this one. Thus, the dream dramatizes the behavior of the real mother, yet it compensates through exaggeration – whereas in reality, we tend to minimize the importance of such things. This could be a call to set more effective boundaries. To this day, for example, Klaus's mother has a key to his apartment so that she can clean up and take care of his laundry. As a divorced man, it is actually very convenient for him, since he does not have to do his housework himself. Perhaps, however, this convenience is no longer appropriate and he ought to give it up. Yet it would be difficult to take such a step. It seems harsh of him to reject his mother's help and support. She does everything voluntarily and cheerfully, and her intentions are actually good.

Since we usually experience care and nurturing as something positive, it can be difficult to say no. Nevertheless, this kind of "no" is part of a continuing process of detachment through which we become increasingly independent of our mothers. Some mothers make this tendency toward autonomy more difficult through more or less open reproaches: they remind their children of their sacrifices and let them know how much gratitude they expect. The wish to be appreciated is in itself quite natural, but when it takes the form of a demand, it can poison a relationship. When it becomes an obligation, gratitude can easily become insincere and it can provoke aggressive fantasies. And the more we feel bound to a particular person, the more easily secret death wishes can develop. Hidden behind such wishes is the hope that merciful destiny will help us to gain the greater independence that we long for. We would simply have to wait patiently and would not incur any guilt on ourselves, because a higher power would solve the problem for us. Such death wishes can be metaphors for a wish for separation; they can be constructive if we are able to understand them as an inner call for more independence. The metaphor of cutting the umbilical cord can also help us understand that a certain amount of aggression is necessary. It will not work without making a cut: this can be painful for both parties involved.

Someone who manages to repress such secret death wishes for his or her entire life might sometimes have nightmares following her mother's death, in which the mother appears again, fit and healthy. The fear of the mother's return – and an irrational fear that she might never have died at all – can trouble the psyche and be processed in a dream. Only waking brings relieved reassurance. Yet such a dream is not entirely incorrect. Even though our mother may be dead in reality, she continues to live in our mother complex and influence our relationships. Someone like Klaus, who dreams of a warlike, invasive mother, might ask himself whether this kind of maternal quality is also at work within him and may be influencing his relationship to himself and to others. Might he be one of those so-called "curling parents" who, in their overdeveloped attitude toward care, run ahead of their children in order to sweep as many obstacles as possible out of the way and provide them with a clear path? He would then be repeating what he experienced in a similar form with his own mother – namely, exaggerated care with a subtle aggressive-destructive aspect.

Twenty-year-old Norbert had an even more unsettling dream:

> I am in the bathroom; I am sitting on the toilet and pushing the flush lever. My mother comes up out of the toilet bowl and grins.

Here, the mother intrudes secretly and invisibly "from below," very close to her son's genital area. What ideas come to mind when something from the "underworld" of the sewer system rises up in one's own toilet? Could it be a demon, a human being or an animal? Because of such fantasies, some people always keep the lid of their toilet closed.

Along with the shock, Norbert also felt terrible disgust. He would have preferred that any animal – even a snake or rat – emerged from the drainpipe rather than his mother. The idea that his mother could see his genitals – perhaps even handle them or bite them – is unbearable. He feels ashamed and helpless, but also very angry. His masculinity and sexuality could be stolen or destroyed by his mother.

As the first woman in his life, a mother unconsciously shapes her son's inner ideas about femininity. From her, he learns what a mother and a woman can be like, and what this means for a man. And in the beginning, the physical relationship between a mother and her son is very intimate. Every mother touches her son's genital area when he is a baby or a toddler – when she bathes him, applies lotion or cleans his bottom. No man can explicitly remember this

123

early sensual contact with the opposite sex, but these experiences continue to have an effect on his unconscious memory.

As he grows older, the son then becomes increasingly aware of his mother's other relationships. Is she completely occupied with her role as a mother, or does she have a job or profession? What kinds of interests and friendships does she have? Does she live alone, in a healthy partnership, or is she discontented, disappointed and reproachful? The more unhappy or bitter a mother is, the more difficult it can be for her to let go of her son. And as soon as he becomes interested in another woman, she is no longer the focal point of his life; instead, she is forced to take a step to the side. In order to compensate for her inner emptiness, in some cases a mother might manipulatively bind her son to herself by devaluing his new partner or increasing his sense of guilt or obligation. However, an excessively close bond with his mother can also originate with a son if he unconsciously idealizes his mother so that she remains the best woman in the world for him in every way.

Norbert interprets the dream as a call to reflect on his relationship with his mother. Even when he reached elementary-school age, she insisted on getting in the bathtub with him, even though this had felt uncomfortable for him for some time. And even now, she seems to come too close to him physically with every greeting. Maybe her attention as a whole is a greater problem than he has acknowledged up to now. But at what point does maternal care become problematic? Andrea had the following dream:

> My mother stands in two places at the same time. One mother is false and evil, but I am not completely sure which one of the two it is. This is horrible.

Aleksandr Solzhenitsyn is convinced that the line which separates good and evil does not lie between nations, social classes or political parties, but straight across every human heart.[110] Accordingly, no human being is exclusively good; rather, each of us consists of one good half and one evil one. This dream, however, describes not only this division but also the difficulty of telling the two apart. What, exactly, is a bad mother and what is a good mother? This is particularly difficult to recognize when we experience a mother as extremely caring. However, an excess of any positive characteristic can become destructive. Too much care and nurturing can be constricting and it can make us dependent. Too much support can make us lazy or increase our feelings of inferiority because we are too out of touch with our own abilities. And if we reverse this example, it becomes clear that even seemingly bad things can have positive aspects. A certain lack of nurturing provides freedom and presents a challenge which can help a child to grow. Nevertheless, good and evil are not always concealed in this way; they are often obvious – as in the case of a violent mother. But even she will have something good hidden away inside of her; she is simply not living it out.

Thus, like Andrea's mother, we are all good as well as evil. Metaphorically speaking, every man has an inner evil brother, and every woman has an inner evil sister. In dreams, these evil sides of ourselves often appear as figures of the same gender and illustrate our destructive potentials. Andrea's mother reminds us that because of our good and bad sides, we are contradictory beings. Therefore, we can very seldom develop unambiguous feelings about ourselves or other people, even if we might fervently wish to do so.

7. Nightmare Motifs from Culture and Technology: When Objects Become Broken or Dangerous

If a bed made of willow branches is buried in the ground, it will grow into a willow tree and not into a bed. Aristotle[111] used this famous example to illustrate a fundamental difference between nature and technology: nature renews itself; technology requires human beings in order to do this. In the beginning there was nature; then human beings arrived on the scene, and only after that came technology. Once upon a time, nature was the most powerful force, and human beings were more powerful than technology. Nowadays, nature is still more powerful than human beings to a great extent – but in certain areas, so is technology. Human beings seem to be stuck in between the two.

The original purpose of culture, rituals and technology was to make people's lives easier and safer, but also to improve upon nature. Accordingly, we could describe a microscope or a telescope as optimized eyes which allow us to see things which are actually invisible to human beings. Ultrasound examinations, magnetic resonance imaging, computer tomography and endoscopy all allow us to cast out the natural darkness. Technology often begins at the point where nature ends, so that we can overcome naturally-occurring limitations rather than accepting them as fated or ordained by God. Through technology, we conquer new living spaces – for example, the sky with airplanes or the ocean with ships. Yet there are dangers associated with this, as Anette's dream demonstrates:

> My brother and I are standing in front of a factory building in the evening, waiting for the bus. Suddenly, a passenger plane crashes down behind the building. I hear loud, violent explosions and screams; I see smoke and fire. Debris flies through the air. We throw ourselves down on the ground.

Airplane Dreams

Human beings are actually terrestrial animals. We can only exist in the water or the air with the aid of technology. In order to survive in these environments which are normally hostile to humans, we require structures: these, however, are fragile and can be broken. Accordingly, Anette asks herself: "What could crash or break and is capable of injuring me?" She has experienced a falling dream, with her dream ego in the observer role.

The section of the air and sky which is close to the earth is the natural habitat of insects and birds; far above this is the place where, according to many religions, God resides. In ancient Greece, the gods lived on Mount Olympus; the Christian God dwells high up in heaven, together with his heavenly host. We do not know who or what God is: nevertheless, this has not prevented human beings in all cultures and since time immemorial from creating images of God. In matter-of-fact terms, these images are projections in which we either believe or do not believe. People have always developed theories and hypotheses related to God. At times of great epochal shifts, images of God often undergo radical changes. Metaphorically speaking, at these times, something can fall from a cosmic height and be shattered. Thus, when something falls down to earth from the vastness of space in a dream, it could mean that religious convictions or set ideas are shattering in the face of earthly reality.

Ultimately, however, not only our metaphysical beliefs and ideas but also all of our scientific theories and hypotheses are constructions of our minds which generally do not last forever. Thus, with the Copernican revolution, human beings had to let go of the idea that the sun revolves around the earth; with Einstein's theory of relativity, they had to reject still other physical absolutes. Here, too, the metaphor of crashing vessels is appropriate, since obsolete theories are shattered theories. As long as they are in place, however, they represent an intact vessel which provides us with orientation and security. The air and the sky, therefore, symbolize the realm of our mind: rational and irrational thoughts and convictions. These also include our respective ideologies and concepts of life. Airplane dreams may be concerned with such concepts or strategies, even if we are not always conscious of them.

Anette has been visiting her brother for several days; she had a fierce argument with him on the evening before the dream. He is annoyed about her very expensive hobby because it prevents her from being able to afford a hotel during her vacation and she is therefore staying with him. From his point of view, she is financing her hobby at his expense. She is appalled at the insinuation that she is taking advantage of his hospitality. The conflict escalates, and each sibling looks for new arguments to convince the other that his or her position is the right one. The tone becomes more and more ferocious, until Anette indignantly locks herself into the guest room. She vows never to visit her brother again.

As the dream illustrates, something actually has been broken as a result of the intense quarrel – and in an unexpected way. Unconscious idealizations may have been shattered. Is her brother perhaps not as happy about her visit as Anette thought he was – or is he in fact envious? And might Anette be more selfish than she would like to admit? The falling pieces of the airplane could represent the ruins that sometimes remain after an argument. In some cases, this kind of rubble can injure everyone involved. When our assumptions or beliefs are broken down, this can be a very painful process; however, it is sometimes a necessary one which can even be freeing and bring us peace.

In my experience, in dreams involving plane crashes, the dream ego is more often in the observer position rather than being a passenger in the airplane. This may have to do with the fact that we *have* a conviction or a theory but we ourselves are not that thing. Many people are capable of abandoning their convictions or letting go of them. However, a person whose dream ego is sitting in a crashing plane may ask him or herself whether she identifies so strongly with a certain idea that with its rejection, she will also be torn apart or destroyed.

Not always, but sometimes it is worth paying attention to the subtle nuances in an airplane dream. Does it make a difference, for example, whether the crashing vehicle is a passenger plane, as in Anette's dream, a private jet, a spaceship, a military plane or a helicopter? Similarly to a passenger plane, which on principle is available to all people, many people within a society share the same convictions and shape the spirit of the times. A private jet belongs to one person alone, meaning that we might have very individual ideas. With a spaceship, we can leave our earthly reality and venture out to new planets and new worlds. If the crashing military plane has been shot down by an enemy, this might draw our attention to a competitive struggle. And if a police or rescue helicopter crashes, the dream might be concerned with internal enforcement of rules or care for our health. However, a circling helicopter might also point toward a relationship between parents and children. Recently, after all, there has been much discussion of "helicopter parents" who continually observe and monitor their children. They limit their children's freedom by constantly wanting to know where they are and what they are doing.

Ships

Nature serves as a model for many technical inventions. An airplane imitates a bird, and ships can be seen as enlarged and improved nutshells. Both things are breakable vessels; this is also the subject of Margot's dream:

I am on a steamship on a wide river, in the midst of a large group of people. We are happy and cheerful. Suddenly there is a great commotion. The ship breaks apart and I have to get onto a little raft. Behind the raft I discover a huge crocodile. The water flows more and more sparsely. I realize with horror that the crocodile is simply waiting for the water to run dry so that it can attack.

In every culture, people have constructed vessels in order to store things. We use them from the beginning of our lives until our deaths – for example: cradles, beds, bowls, cupboards or coffins. In this sense, even apartments, houses and clothing have the quality of vessels. Therefore, what difference does it make in a dream, whether a person is being carried by a donkey or by a ship? Fundamentally, the donkey is a part of nature whereas the ship is human-made. If, in a dream, the donkey you are riding collapses, you could ask yourself what part of nature is refusing to work. Is it obstinacy, stubbornness – or your own body, which can no longer tolerate the burden? When a ship breaks apart, a carrier of culture is destroyed. What societal frameworks might be breaking? Where do you no longer belong? Within society, we belong to different cultural worlds – not always with clear separation: in the world of children or of adults; in the world of the well-off or of the needy; in the world of the employed or of retirees; in the world of the healthy or of the sick. Someone who falls overboard in a dream might sometimes be experiencing a not-so-gentle reminder that he or she could fall out of one of these frameworks. Like Margot, we sometimes have to change vessels along our journey through life and find our way by makeshift or provisional means.

Due to a severe illness, Margot has dropped out of the world of the healthy. We can experience what it is like to be sick when we have a bad stomach flu or a migraine attack. Weakness and pain shut us out from daily life. We cannot sit at a table and eat together with other people; we might not even be able to take a shower, and we certainly cannot work. We are exiled. But once we have recovered, our past misery can sometimes seem unreal or scarcely imaginable.

Shortly after being diagnosed with Parkinson's disease, the sociology professor Helmut Dubiel had recurring dreams about ships.[112] He dreamed about a steamship on the ocean, filled with laughing, happy people. During the night, he was thrown overboard. The steamer sailed rapidly ahead, leaving him behind. This image illustrates how a severe illness can isolate the affected person. While the healthy people sail onward, happily remaining on course, the sick person is not only under threat from the forces of nature, but he is completely on his own. Both the raft in Margot's dream and Helmut Dubiel's swimming also remind us that illness significantly slows the tempo of our lives.

There are many things that we can no longer do as quickly as we could when we were healthy; but the illness itself also demands our time and attention.

Elvira's dream depicts another dangerous scenario aboard a ship:

> I am running around on a ship which is about to sink. There are bombs below deck which could explode. It is frightening.

Elvira generally avoids conflicts. She does not like arguments, either at home or at her workplace. She generally makes an effort to assuage tensions or to minimize them. Even though Elvira does not like her daughter-in-law at all, she gave her a box of "Mon Cheri" chocolates (the name means "my darling") on the evening before the dream.

A bomb contains explosive materials and explosive power. It is designed for battle and war. Numerous proverbs refer to the nature of bombs. For example, if something is "bombproof," it is resistant to all kinds of abuse. However, when someone "drops a bomb," they reveal something alarming or unexpected. On the other hand, if we say something is "a bomb," we mean that it is superlatively wonderful; if "business is booming," then it is a great success.

Bombs can also rise up in our psyches – for instance, when we constantly swallow and repress our aggravation. We cannot get rid of it in this way: instead, it piles up unconsciously and condenses into rage. At some point, a trivial occurrence is enough to ignite the bomb. The explosion discharges all of the old aggression in one stroke.

Elvira is also familiar with this. For years now, she has swallowed the annoyance and resentment she feels toward her daughter-in-law and tried as best she can to remain polite and friendly. And as usual, the dinner together passed without any outward incident. But could it be that she overdid it with the gift of chocolates. "Mon Cheri" represents the exact opposite of her true feelings; thus, the gift is absolutely insincere. The tension between her inner feelings and her outward behavior could hardly be greater. Under conditions such as these, bombs are likely to emerge. Elvira would like to forget the dream as quickly as possible, but in doing so, she would miss the chance to confront feelings of aggression which are in danger of spinning out of control.

Traveling

All of life is a journey; therefore it is not surprising that in our dreams we are often traveling – whether on foot or using modern transportation, like Waltraut:

> I am in a completely overcrowded train, and I am looking for the toilet. I walk through many, many cars, but there is no toilet anywhere. I begin to panic.

What do you associate with train travel? Do you enjoy this comfortable form of traveling, or do you become irritated because trains are often overcrowded, dirty or do not run on time. Do you only use trains occasionally or not at all because you can travel more independently with a car? Depending on your real traveling habits, a dream will shed light on different things.

At the most general level, we are flexible when we drive a car, whereas a train, as a collective means of transportation, travels on preset tracks from which it cannot deviate. Figuratively speaking, traveling by train in a dream may therefore have something to do with routine practices, standards or predetermined norms. However, normality is not only common; it is also frequently advantageous. After all, we belong to the middle of society – since by definition, a norm is an average value. If we behave normally like everyone else, we will also have the impression that our behavior is correct and orderly.

In her dream, Waltraut knows that all of the other passengers want to get to the same place as quickly as possible. Might she then have a personal goal which she shares with many other people? Is there a societal trend that she is also following? Anxious about the financial crisis and concerned about the depreciation of currency, Waltraut would like to invest the money she has inherited in a residential property. Her concerns about monetary stability are, in fact, something which she shares with many other people – as is the idea of investing her fortune in real estate. Consequently, however, the particularly attractive and affordable properties have become scarce, especially in desirable locations.

If Waltraut's dream refers to her search for a condominium, then it is clear that she is not happy with her situation at present. In fact, she has already been searching intensively for two years, but she has not been successful. In the dream as well, she cannot find a place to satisfy her natural needs.

The toilet is the place we look for when we need to relieve ourselves of something. We can postpone this for a certain amount of time, but at some point we are no longer able to do so because nature takes over. Then we lose control over ourselves. What happens now? In her imagination, Waltraut starts from the end of her dream and looks for an appropriate solution to her problem. She could continue to look for a toilet in other parts of the train for a while longer and simply not give up hope. Maybe the train will stop at the next station soon, and she can get out. In the worst-case scenario, she could jump from the moving train or activate the emergency brake.

Two days before her dream, Waltraut fell and fractured her lower arm. Because of this, she missed an appointment to view a condominium. She was thwarted by an accident, and her frustration with the complicated search for an apartment is steadily growing. She interprets the dream as a reflection of her unsatisfying situation – but also as a call to pause and reflect. Is it simply a matter of being a little more patient – that is, continuing to do what she has done up to now? Would it make sense to rethink her search criteria, such as the location and size of the property? Does the kind of property she has been looking for so far really correspond to her personal needs? Or might it even be better not to invest in a condominium at all, even though many people are currently doing this? Sometimes we "jump on a moving train" because we want to get our share of something good; but it is equally possible that we need to jump off the bandwagon in order to find another, more appropriate path for ourselves.

Trains and railway travel are frequent dream motifs. Someone who is desperately trying, but failing, to disembark from a train might ask him or herself in what collective trend he could be caught up. On the other hand, someone who misses a train in a dream could ask herself in what area of society she might not be keeping up or might have missed a connection. This dream motif helped a 60-year-old man to recognize his fear of losing his job. Unlike his younger colleagues, he had difficulty coping with the constant restructuring taking place in his firm. With his slow and laborious pace, he felt increasingly overwhelmed and unsure of himself, while his colleagues seemed to be outpacing him.

Thus, being left behind instead of moving forward and coming along with others would be a subject of the dream motif of missing a train. This can often be a terrible feeling. Yet in reality, we occasionally hear about people who, for unforeseeable reasons, have missed a train and by doing so avoid being involved in an accident. Therefore it can be worth asking ourselves under what conditions it could be advantageous for us not to catch our train in a dream.

Perhaps missing the train will turn out to be a good thing, even if it seemed terrible at first glance. For example, a woman dreamed that she did not manage to board a train before it left the station, even though her husband was already on board. Following her initial shock at the idea that they were no longer traveling together on the same track, the dreamer felt a sense of satisfaction. She had spent many years supporting her husband in building up his business, but now it was time for her to reawaken her own professional interests.

When we use public transportation, we do not steer the vehicle ourselves, as we do when we drive a car or ride a bicycle. Bettina's dream deals with this subject:

> I am traveling – sometimes on foot, sometimes in my car, then by bus. The latter drives very close to the ocean; the waves are strong and they come close to the bus. Some people are anxious, but I have the feeling that the driver knows what he is doing. The waves wash through underneath the bus; the ocean is unpredictable. Suddenly, the water is up to my neck; then it is over my head and I wake up in a panic and take a deep breath.

In her dream, Bettina changes her mode of transportation. First, she travels on foot, using her own strength. Then she drives in her own car before transferring to the bus. Now she is no longer steering, but she puts her trust in the bus driver, and like every passenger, she assumes that he is well-rested, competent and a careful driver. However, she is mistaken in her assessment, and he seems to underestimate the power of the ocean. If Bettina interprets the bus driver as an inner aspect of her personality, then the dream is concerned with where or in whom she can place her trust when confronted with natural forces.

In her real life, Bettina has had an affair; it is essential that her jealous and hot-tempered husband does not find out about it. He would be capable of anything: therefore she has very carefully and skillfully kept her affair a secret. Now the dream toys with the possibility that she could be overcome by the tide. Does the dream simply reflect her suppressed fear – or could she actually get into a dangerous situation? What might come crashing over her like a wave? Is the dream concerned with violent feelings on her own part – or those of her lover or her husband – which she has underestimated?[113] For some time, Bettina has felt quite comfortable in this love triangle, and she does not actually wish to change anything. Because of the dream, she now has the feeling that perhaps she has settled in too well and does not want to acknowledge how explosive the situation could become. The dream tells of the power of water, but Bettina considers the motif of fire to be more fitting: she asks herself if she is currently playing with fire. The solution to which the dream points is the following: take a deep breath and reassess. From this point of view, the dream can be seen as a warning against excessive naiveté and hubris.

Rooms and Buildings

Occasionally we are even traveling inside our own houses, as in the case of Sigrid:

> I go down into the basement to clear out some old papers and cardboard packaging. As I am coming downstairs, I discover father; he has brought me some wood and is stacking it. He moves very quietly because he does not want to be noticed. I am startled when I see him. One level further down in the basement is an emaciated, feral black bear; it tries to come upstairs. Father tries to push it back down with a rake, but it is nearly hopeless. From even further below, I hear screams and strange noises. I want to run away, to go back upstairs, but I cannot move from where I am.

Up until a few decades ago, disobedient children were locked in basements as a punishment. Even some adults dislike going into basements because they are damp, cold and dark. Others are afraid of mice, spiders or rats. A basement is also a place that can make our flesh creep – not only because of such real conditions, but also because it can greatly arouse our imagination. What sorts of things might be hiding down there that we do not know about? Are there monsters lurking – or dead bodies, or animals? Do we suspect something dangerous or mysterious? For the very reason that a basement makes many people feel afraid, it can also be a good place for secret meetings or be used as a hiding place. Furthermore, we still use basements as a place to store old or seldom-used objects or junk – but also reserve supplies or occasionally something valuable. It is similar to our unconscious mind. Alongside forgotten or repressed subjects (Germans speak of "corpses in the cellar" – equivalent to the English expression "skeletons in the closet"), there may also lie resources of which we could take advantage. Thus, it is hardly surprising that basements in dreams often symbolize our unconscious – and also sometimes our sexual organs – and the things that happen there can sometimes make us uneasy.

The very nature of a basement space can provide some insights into the unconscious regions of our psyche. Someone who encounters air raid shelters or bunkers might consider what he or she needs protection from. Perhaps it is unbearable battles and arguments in everyday life that trigger a wish for a place of retreat. Sometimes dusty, ancient rooms from the Middle Ages or even earlier times may suddenly appear in our dreams. Here, we may have penetrated a deep layer of the psyche – the so-called collective unconscious, which extends beyond our personal memories into long-distant human experience. Finally, someone who encounters brand new basement spaces might ask him or herself what previously unseen aspects of his unconscious are now coming into view. However, while some people feel curious about such new rooms, others may react with fear, depending upon whether we experience the unknown as enriching or suspicious.

If we expect to find something alarming in our dream basement and we refuse to descend any further, it is often still too early to face up to these repressed experiences or to something unknown. Instead of continuing on and becoming overwhelmed, it is better for us to turn back. Occasionally, however, we cannot run away at all, perhaps because our legs are suddenly shackled or we are glued to the spot, like Sigrid. Initially, she wants to tidy up on the first level of the basement – a dream motif which often refers to an internal process of clarification and dawning awareness. Just as we clear old papers out of the basement in real life, we can also sort out those repressed experiences that lie close to our consciousness, evaluate them, and dispose of unnecessary old burdens. In the process, something unexpected can sometimes turn up.

In Sigrid's case, her father and the neglected bear appear; but initially, she does not wish to face either of these figures. However, the dream thwarts her escape from her father who, when she was a child, humiliated her and called her a dummy because of her dyslexia. Perhaps the dream will provide her with the courage to give up her tendency to flee: after all, Sigrid is no longer a helpless child, and she is actually capable of confronting her old, habitual patterns of behavior. Furthermore, she cannot really flee from her father, since she long ago unconsciously internalized him and his tendency to put her down. Even without being physically present, he has continued to affect her as her internal father, and over the course of many years, he has probably cut her off from her "bear-like" strengths. Now this inner father seems to no longer possess the proper tools to ward off the neglected bear. Here, Sigrid might be called upon to act: her inner bear must be fed and cared for so that it can regain its strength and be available to her as an inner life force. This is not without its dangers, since the bear's wild strength could lead to some turmoil in her life. But it also appears that Sigrid needs to revise her one-sided image of her father. By supplying her with wood, he is making natural energy available to her, and she can benefit from this.

Progressing further and moving on are subjects frequently associated with the dream motif of stairs. Perhaps we simply do not dare to step onto a staircase; maybe it is buried or in need of repair. Its length, its steepness, the type of steps and the banisters are all decisive factors as to whether we can or want to use the staircase at all. Sometimes, a staircase in a dream suddenly comes to an end – or it has no banisters, or it moves around in space. Someone who finds him or herself in the midst of such uncomfortable dream images might consider whether she is currently in a difficult situation of transition in her real life. After all, stairways and ladders are connecting routes through which we can overcome a difference in elevation between two places. We are not at home on a staircase; rather, we are in a transitional space: we have already left the old location, but we have not yet arrived at a new one. If a stairway or a ladder then breaks off on our way up, this could, for example, refer to a planned ascension up the career ladder or some other development or upward movement which is not possible at the moment. On the other hand, someone standing on a staircase or ladder which ends several meters before reaching the ground might question him or herself about his current sense of groundedness or contact with reality. Whereas in such a situation, some people should jump down in order to keep their feet on the firm ground of reality, for some realists, this signal could indicate: Concrete facts are not everything. Explore the world of fantasies, wishes or longings!

Yet even an intact staircase can become a problem: for example, if we walk up or down without arriving anywhere. This could raise the question of whether we even recognize or are able to find a goal. For some people this is distressing; others experience it as pleasant not to have to linger in one place. In some cases, however, we have to climb too many steps, so that our strengths are exhausted before we even reach our goal. Since this problem also exists in the real world, engineers invented elevators which can transport us comfortably and quickly. Nevertheless, not everyone is convinced of their advantages over stairways. In reality, some people do not like to ride in elevators because they are frightened by the thought of getting stuck – for example, in the case of a power failure. Comfort and speed come at a price: for a short period of time, we must allow ourselves to be enclosed and at the mercy of technology. Leonie's short dream illustrates this:

I am trapped inside an elevator. I scream, but no one can hear me.

The elevator in Leonie's dream is ascending a large administration building – her workplace. Thus, she is trapped in the place that is concerned with her professional position and professional relationships. Here, she seems to be isolated, with no support or room to maneuver. No one notices her, and her screams die away: a classic situation of workplace bullying, with a helpless, marginalized victim. Since in the dream, there is no evident solution to her problem, expert knowledge might be called for in order to develop solutions to this hopeless situation. Then, metaphorically speaking, Leonie would be empowered to open the elevator door and reclaim her freedom of movement.

In dreams, doors may even be completely missing, so that it is impossible to leave or enter a certain place. As dreamers faced with this motif, we could ask ourselves whether there might be concrete or psychological situations which we cannot escape or where we are not allowed to enter. In dreams, doors often symbolize possibilities for connections or encounters. For example, we say someone's "door is always open" if one enjoys welcoming others and shows herself to be a hospitable person. On the other hand, houses with locked doors and closed shutters are a sign that someone wants to remain undisturbed. A need for security might also be a relevant theme here.

Someone who feels threatened in a dream by doors that are too wide open or cannot be locked may be called upon to examine a shortage or lack of possibilities for setting boundaries in his or her life and to deal with his need for protection. It can be similar if a door key is lost or stolen: the "power of the keys" is missing, and with it, our power and influence over rooms. Without keys, we cannot enter certain rooms, nor can we lock them. Faced with a relationship conflict in his real life, Andreas is also unable to open a door in his dream:

> I am in a room with a white door. My wife is on the other side. I try to push the door open in order to reach her. She pushes back against it. The door grows higher and higher. I cry out, "Dear God, help me!" and continue to push against the

door. The more I exert myself, the taller and heavier it becomes. Suddenly the door begins to fall down onto me from above.

In the dream, Andreas is trying to reach his wife, from whom he is separated only by a door. However, the two have set their strengths against each other in an unrelenting relationship conflict. This could be a warning: Andreas's means of trying to save the relationship elicit enormous resistance form his partner. Regardless of whether he is reacting to her with too much pressure, too many demands, or in some other way: if his mode of behavior remains the same – according to the dream – he will never be able to reach his partner. Furthermore, he will not only lose out in the power struggle, but he will also do damage to himself as a result of his efforts, since the increasingly heavy door is threatening to crush him.

What could this mean concretely for Andreas, who wants to save his marriage at all costs? It would probably be helpful for him to tell his wife about the dream and ask her whether she recognizes these dream images in her current relationship situation. Perhaps she will be taken aback by the way Andreas's unconscious depicts the partnership. If the dream seems accurate from her point of view, she might be able to identify the reasons for her resistance, and possibly even be able to say what actions or behavior on Andreas's part would allow her to open the door. However, she might also admit to him that she intends to keep the door to the relationship closed because she is already working on plans for a future in which Andreas no longer has a place. In other words, a discussion of the dream might allow the couple to describe their relationship conflict in symbolic terms and to formulate their ideas about a future, either together or apart, in metaphorical images using the door.

Connections between people are possible not only through doors, but also via telephones, smart phones or computers. Dreams in which these devices are broken, stolen or lost can leave us with a horrible feeling of being cut off or isolated. A person who is familiar with this dream motif might consider to what degree his or her contact and exchange of information with other people might be impaired. Sometimes, however, a subject-level perspective is more appropriate, since the connection to our own interior world has been broken off. Whenever we lose the connection to our own feelings, fantasies or needs, in a metaphorical sense, a line of transmission to our inner world has been disrupted.

Thus, the flow of information can run dry either in the direction of the outside world or in that of our spiritual world. However, only the concrete circumstances of the dreaming person's life can show us whether such an interruption of contact is detrimental or helpful. Someone who is inundated with external or internal impressions sometimes needs to disconnect the lines of communication for a certain period of time in order to regenerate. In the case of the dream motif of a door, this could also mean that not every door ought to be opened. Something destructive or frightening might also be hiding behind a door, as we see in Lena's dream:

> I am in an attic with two directly adjoining rooms. Each room contains a gas stove. One stove, which belongs to my grandmother, is burning. The other one – a modern stove – is leaking gas. As soon as the door connecting the two rooms is opened, there is an explosion.

Similarly to the basement, other rooms can also serve as symbols of our inner psychological world or our bodies. Here, the levels or stories of a building sometimes correspond to the different layers of our psyches or different physical levels. Top floors or attics often have to do with something that is happening in our heads: they represent the world of thoughts, of reason or of spirituality. If Lena's dream refers to her psychological world, something dangerous might be brewing there.

Like our thoughts, the gas in the dream is primarily invisible. In addition, it is flammable: thus, we speak of "the spark of an idea" that fires us up or inspires us. In Christianity, the Holy Spirit is described not only using the symbol of wind, but also with the symbol of a flame. These images indicate that psychological phenomena possess a potential for energy and power which we can clearly sense in the form of enthusiasm or excitement. When we are inspired, we experience the energizing power of an idea or an ideology. Thus, we can be fueled or stimulated not only by a physical impulse, but also by intellect, reasoning or spirituality. And like any fire, a psychological fire can have a warming as well as a destructive effect. A look back into history attests to this at the collective level. More than a few leaders have inspired nations with their ideas; yet they have also left behind a great deal of scorched earth – both in a concrete sense and in the souls of human beings.

Ideas can light a fire under an entire nation or a single individual, as Lena's dream of the two gas stoves indicates. Since the burning gas stove belongs to her grandmother, she might ask herself whether her grandmother's beliefs – particularly those related to femininity, womanhood and motherliness – have an unconscious effect on her. If she discovers these ideas within herself, the dream could be correcting her self-image by pointing out that even she, as a modern woman, has still not overcome the attitudes of her parents or her grandparents. Accordingly, there would still be a room inside of her where the spiritual values of her grandmother reside – as well as a second room whose modern stove more closely represents the values of the contemporary zeitgeist.

In Lena's case, the meeting of these contrasting sets of values seems to have quite an explosive potential. She is currently experiencing such a clash of incompatible values in the context of her unwanted pregnancy: Must I carry this baby to term because, from a Christian perspective, an unborn child's right to life is indisputable? Or can I have an abortion because a child would interfere with my plans for the future? How egotistical do I have the right to be? A person who exposes herself to the tension between two such conflicting positions can sometimes be nearly torn apart on the inside.

Lena's dream demonstrates that it can be worth paying attention to whether any objects or pieces of furniture in our dreams originated with our family members or ancestors and therefore might indicate that their concepts of life remain psychologically relevant for us. In a sense, we not only possess furnishings for

143

our real-life homes, but we are also psychologically "furnished." Sometimes it takes a dream to make us consciously aware of the degree and form in which traditions influence us psychologically. For example, someone who dreams of being in his or her parents' or grandparents' bathroom or bed might be much more greatly influenced by their elders' traditional values regarding intimacy or sexuality than he would like to admit. However, wardrobes, cars or certain utensils belonging to our parents might also reveal previously hidden areas where their psychological influence shapes our current lives.

Machines, Equipment and Appliances

Many machines and appliances simplify our lives – for example, by saving us time or physical effort. Yet these advantages also have their drawbacks, as Helga's dream demonstrates:

I am steering a truck; my little son Julian sits in the passenger seat. Suddenly, two men pull him out of the car. I am frozen with fear; I remain sitting motionless. When Julian suddenly reappears, he is five kilograms lighter and fuzzy like an animal because he has been washed and spun in the washing machine. That was torture.

Helga wakes up shaken and ashamed because in her dream, she was not able to protect her only son, now four years old, from the kidnappers. Furthermore, in reality she has never driven a truck, and she is therefore amazed at how easily and confidently she was able to steer such a large vehicle in her dream. However, since in her professional life she is very successful in a male-dominated field, travels often and is granted a lot of freedom, steering a truck is certainly a fitting metaphor for her professional skill and her work situation. Yet it is not Helga herself, but her son who is put in danger. He is the victim of a kidnapping. If the unknown abductors represent inner aspects of Helga herself, it would be worth examining what unconscious predatory forces are at work in her, and what it might mean to put something or someone into a washing machine.

Julian goes to a nursery during the day, and he is quite happy there. The only problem is that he is tired and moves slowly in the mornings when he has to eat breakfast, wash and get dressed. Helga sometimes feels forced to deal rather roughly with his dawdling. It also annoys her that she is already rushed and under stress in the mornings because of Julian's behavior – even though she normally has no trouble being well organized herself. Due to her son's playfulness, it is only with great effort that she usually manages to leave the house on time.

For small children, it is not always easy to start the day quickly early in the morning. The strict schedules and time divisions of the modern professional world can run contrary to children's natural rhythm. Whereas many adults have not only internalized such demands but have long since accepted them, in the case of children, something is taken away – or stolen – from them. In the dream scenario, these demands were personified by the kidnappers, who did not steal the adult but only the child.

Time management which is economically advantageous for adults becomes a burden for real children, but also for our so-called "inner child," when things like playfulness, spontaneity or leisure time are given short shrift due to economic demands. Symbolically, this economical and efficient time structure could be represented by the image of a washing machine. With its standardized washing cycles, a washing machine embodies, among other things, the principle of efficiency and saving time.

Helga's dream might be saying that while these cultural achievements may not be destroying her son's existence, they may be placing a large amount of strain on him – since the washing machine cycle does not care for him in the intended manner; rather it "dishevels" him. Thus, Julian most certainly does not benefit from the use of the washing machine; in fact, it is damaging to him.

The washing machine might represent Helga's attempts to make it clear to Julian that he needs to move more quickly in the mornings, since the dream motifs of washing and cleaning very often represent our attempts at order and clarity. Similarly to freshly-cleaned windows which provide us with a clear view, a psychological cleansing can help us to see internal phenomena more clearly. For example, when we say that something has become "clear" to us, we are speaking of new-found insights or connections which have been clarified.

Cleaning is also an important motif in Charlotte's dream:

> A woman wakes me up and wants me to clean her business premises immediately. But it is the middle of the night, about 1 a.m. I go into the office building, first into the cafeteria; the light is very bright and harsh. The room is ice cold, like a refrigerator. The room almost seems like it is under construction. There are white "frost flowers" on the windows. Several television sets are running; they are supposed to provide warmth. It is a very eerie, spooky atmosphere.

The motif of sleeping in a dream reminds us that we are actually subject to natural phenomena which repeat in a rhythmic cycle – such as the ebb and flow of tides, as well as the menstrual cycle, the phases of the moon or the seasons. As early as the fifteenth century, Paracelsus recommended that people go to bed when darkness falls and get up again at sunrise because he believed that adherence to the rhythms of day and night was beneficial to our health.

This type of attitude has become completely foreign to us, since technology has freed us to a great extent from these periodic natural processes. Today, for example, we can turn the night into day with electric lighting or use medication to modify hormonal cycles or rhythms of sleeping and waking according to our wishes. Nevertheless, up to now we have not succeeded in doing away with sleep – even though, in periods when time is increasingly short, valuable reserves of time are lying unused here. After all, someone who sleeps for eight hours is unavailable either for productive activity or scientific thinking for one third of the day. Dreams in which sleep or sleep disturbances play a central role may thus be concerned with the conflict between our natural need for regeneration and our desire for the power to do away with sleep. According to Peter von Matt,[114] the fact that we do not have mastery over sleep is the subtlest and most ancient insult to humanity.

Sleep, however, is a state of unconsciousness. If, for example, we say to someone: "Wake up already!" we are demanding that he or she look or listen more consciously. We want the person to finally recognize what is going on. In order to do so, she must be awake, present and attentive. And just as a real person can summon us to be more conscious, a dream can do so as well. In Charlotte's dream, the unknown woman is probably an inner aspect of her personality which wakes her up and gives her the task of cleaning the office space. Since, as we have already mentioned, cleaning also often symbolizes clarification and gaining awareness, Charlotte might be motivated to reflect on her professional situation. The dream takes her to the cafeteria – to the place where co-workers eat together during breaks and where they cultivate their relationships. Even in a business that does not have an actual cafeteria, a symbolic cafeteria might actually exist: this would be the nourishing "place" that an employer makes available and also frequently subsidizes.

In the dream, this office cafeteria is unpleasantly cold and uninviting. With these images as a starting point, Charlotte might ask herself, in the most general sense, what nourishing and maternal qualities the company management displays. Does the executive level tend to be frosty and ungenerous toward the employees? Does it, in fact, cultivate an atmosphere of fear or mistrust? Does it poison relationships between colleagues? And what might it say about Charlotte's workplace that heat is supposed to be generated by something as completely inappropriate as television sets?

However, the unpleasant situation is not hopeless. There is hope because the cafeteria in the dream is still under construction – it is still being formed. Similar to the new construction or renovation of a real house, there are also psychological processes of building and redesigning. A new construction or a renovation in our interior world or in interpersonal relationships often points to a potential for change. The situation is not entrenched; it can be reshaped or formed anew. Such dreams about construction sites are particularly encouraging when we are longing for a change or when a change is urgently necessary.

Appliances, machines and technology have also become indispensable in the field of medicine, since they allow us to overcome natural processes and strokes of fate. Nevertheless, some of the advantages brought by medical achievements are not always easy to cope with psychologically.

For example, in his autobiographical account, *Deep in the Brain* (German: *Tief im Hirn*),[115] sociology professor Helmut Dubiel describes how, as a treatment for his advanced Parkinson's disease, a depth electrode was implanted in his brain. The operation triggered nightmares as well as a nightmare-like fantasy: Dubiel saw himself as a dog who must tolerate the attack of a chainsaw on its doghouse. This violent image symbolizes what it means to put one's own body at the mercy of a surgeon and his equipment – even when the procedure is sensible, beneficial and desired.

In addition, the result of every successful operation must be tolerable: this is especially challenging if the operation alters our previous identity. Helmut Dubiel has had this experience, since a transmitter allows him to turn the depth electrode implanted in his brain on and off. As soon as he sends an electrical stimulus to the affected region of his brain, the trembling and disturbed movements brought on by his Parkinson's illness are significantly alleviated. At the same time, the electrical impulse impairs his ability to speak to such a degree that he is unable to deliver a lecture. Only when he deactivates the electrode does this side effect disappear, and Professor Dubiel is able to teach again. Then, however, he is no longer able to walk.

This example demonstrates that we are no longer limited to maintaining our inborn biological identity, but we can also become a hybrid creature that is part living thing and part machine – a cyborg (or cybernetic organism).[116] When a foreign body becomes a part of us, we must integrate it into our physical and psychological beings and somehow come to grips with our altered self. The integration of alien elements into our own bodies can evoke similar psychological reactions to that of the integration of foreigners into our external world: we might be relaxed or disinterested; or we could be fascinated, frightened or perhaps overwhelmed.[117] Even a cardiac pacemaker challenges us to welcome a small device into our bodies and allow it to take over the regulation of our hearts. However, since it simply replaces an unreliable natural process and does not otherwise change us in any way, this causes little distress to most patients.

A person who owes his or her life to technology will often develop a positive attitude toward technical possibilities. Thus, a young woman regularly awoke with pleasant feelings following dreams about deserted laboratories and glass cases. Despite her fundamentally open-minded attitude toward technology, she was astonished by these positive feelings. Only when she remembered that she would not have survived the childbirth process without the help of medical technology, did this make sense to her. Now, for the first time, she felt a deep and conscious sense of gratitude toward medical technology, which had saved her life after nature had forsaken her.

Given the increasing technization of daily life, our dreams are also likely to pick up more and more on the subject of technology and help us to more consciously understand its significance in the shaping of our individual lives.

The Supremacy of Technology

Nightmares do not necessarily refer to our personal life circumstances, as the following dream illustrates:

> I am in Japan, and I see a vast, open landscape. I am all alone and it is quiet. Suddenly I feel as if the war has just ended. It is a terrible feeling.

Herbert wakes up in a terrible panic; during the day he has great difficulty concentrating. The nightmare seems completely inexplicable to him, since he has no relationship to the country or the people who live there. He has no idea what Japan might symbolize for him personally. A few days later, on March 11, 2011, when a nuclear catastrophe takes place in the Japanese city of Fukushima, Herbert suspects that his unconscious mind somehow "anticipated" the accident. If this is correct, the dream would have contained a coded reference to a future, collectively significant event. Although the phenomenon is not scientifically provable, this would then be one of many prospective dreams which hint at coming events.

A prospective dream is comparable to an intuition which suddenly gives us an apprehension of the future in a waking state. Not only is it unclear why we are experiencing such a foreboding, but we must also wait until the anticipated event actually occurs – since we can only be certain in retrospect whether we actually had a premonition or simply wishful thinking. But are there actually any clues to the reactor failure in Herbert's dream? The postwar period indicated at the end of his dream could remind us of the first collective catastrophe resulting from the use of the atomic bomb. However, the discrepancy that Herbert describes between his intense feeling of panic and the harmless images – which, in contrast to the real situation in Japan, do not depict any concrete destruction – seems significant.

Nevertheless, after the tsunami, the greatest threat – namely, the radioactivity – was invisible to everyone. We cannot smell or hear nuclear radiation either. None of our sensory organs are capable of recognizing it. In other words, nature did not intend for us to be able to detect it.[118] If the dream refers to the radioactivity released in Fukushima, therefore, Herbert's panic would certainly be appropriate. After all, it is the hidden, secret power of radioactivity that makes it so sinister and dreadful. In the absence of measuring instruments, we remain ignorant and can only believe the official measurements and statements of the authorities.

Nowadays, many people have lost faith in the idea that nuclear technology can remain controllable. Fukushima has shown us that not only nature, but also technology can get out of our control. Today, people can become victims of unbridled natural and technological forces. Thus, technology possesses a destructive potential which is equal to that of nature, as the following dream indicates:

> I am standing in the garden at night and looking at the starry sky. A stream of flashing, lighted dots appears to my right – like greatly magnified, sparkling stars that are moving toward me. The stream comes closer and closer and consumes the entire sky. Between all of the flashing lights, I see a meteor streak across the sky and I think "Yes, that is a real shooting star." That was what I had been looking for. Then the flashing of the little points becomes more intense and harsh. I realize that these little particles are not meteors; rather, they are made by human beings and are being used to wage war.

Shooting stars are small meteors which burn up when they enter the earth's atmosphere and delight many people with their flashing light. Our enjoyment of falling stars is due not only to the natural spectacle in the night sky, but probably also to an old tradition which says that when we see a shooting star we are allowed to make a wish. This belief links heavenly phenomena with human longings which we hope will become reality. When we consider that in many religions, the gods influence life on earth from the vantage point of the sky – or that people read their fortunes in the constellations, this idea is actually not unusual. For thousands of years, people have been projecting their hopes as well as their fears onto the cosmos, its powers and the events that take place in the skies. Yet the once "divine" cosmos is increasingly becoming a demystified space which human beings are conquering with their technical equipment, for beneficial as well as destructive purposes. Not only do we launch satellites into the earth's orbit in order to study the weather and transmit news and information, but we also use the skies for military purposes.

It is not only the latter which the dreamer recognizes at the end of her dream; she also sees a certain similarity between natural phenomena and modern warfare technology. This is certainly plausible, since there are people who watch sheet lightening, a solar eclipse or meteor showers with great fascination; at the same time, there are those who direct enormous enthusiasm and fascination toward the development of aircraft to be used for combat purposes.

The destructive potential that exists within technology is relevant not only for this dreamer, but for all of humankind. It seems that with such nightmares, we share the burden of the terrible things that happen in this world on a daily basis.

Conclusion

What can we do when we no longer feel at home in our own inner world, because our psyche is sending us nightmares? This book raises that core question: however, it does not claim to provide a complete or unequivocal answer. The book has already achieved its goal if it has made readers curious about exploring the meaning of their own frightening nocturnal scenarios in order to take advantage of the hidden resources that these nightmares contain. At the same time, addressing the dark abysses of our inner beings in this way can deepen our knowledge of ourselves and the world and strengthen our capacity to cope with terrible experiences.

The artist Max Ernst once said: "When an artist finds himself, he is lost! Heaven help him if he wants to know what he wants!"[119] With these words, in my opinion, Ernst underscored the importance of the unconscious for the creative process. Conscious understanding would be disruptive, because it gives the artist distance; it catapults him or her outside of the immediate experience and spares him from concern as well as from suffering.

Only when human intellect is not sufficient to understand our nightmare scenarios – and this does happen, because nightmares represent ambiguous experiences – are we forced to deal with the unknown, an action that Max Ernst undertook voluntarily in the service of his art. In the case of such nightmares, it can be a matter of seeking out a supportive foundation and the security that allows us to tolerate the dreadful experience.

Appendix 1:

Index of key words in the nightmare motifs

The following nightmare motifs are discussed in this book with the help of sample dreams. They must be understood within the personal life context of each respective dreamer; therefore, their interpretation is only intended to provide the reader with points of reference.

155

Appendix 2:

Understanding your own nightmare motifs

Every dream is unique. Therefore, it is entirely possible that the dream examples discussed here will not provide you with sufficient help in understanding your own individual nightmare. The following set of questions is designed to encourage you to pay attention to ideas, facts, images or memories so that you may come a little closer to understanding the meaning of your nightmare.

1. Place your focus on yourself – on your so-called dream ego:

- Do you perhaps not appear at all in your dream? Do you remain at a distance, in the observer role, or are you involved in the action of the dream?
- Do you behave actively in the dream, or are you a passive recipient of the action?
- Do you behave appropriately or clumsily in the face of the threat/fear/atrocity? In other words: when is your dream ego skillful, strong or powerful, and when is the dream ego weak, foolish or naive?
- Is your behavior in the dream foreign or embarrassing to you – or are you amazed because you dare or are able to do something that you would find impossible in real life?

157

These questions will help you get to know various facets of your dream ego which, in a second step, you can compare with the ego you know in reality. Try to figure out the reasons for any possible discrepancies between your dream ego and your real ego:

- What does this difference feel like?
- What does the difference make you aware of?
- What is the significance of the dream ego's situation for your current real-life situation?

2. Now place your focus on the relationship experiences in the dream:

- Are there relationships between people and other living things, with nature or perhaps with God?
- Is the dream ego alone or isolated?
- What is the quality of the relationships in the dream? Are they characterized by affection, trust and respect – or are the dominant qualities distance, power, oppression, destruction or even annihilation?
- Is competition or cooperation more dominant in your dream?
- What ideas occur to you with regard to these relationship experiences? What comes up for you when you compare them with the qualities of relationships in your waking life? Do you encounter something typical or atypical? What significance does this have for your current living situation?

3. Take a closer look at the type of threat or danger:

- What is the source of the threat or danger in the dream? Is it nature, human beings, technology or something else?
- Is your dream ego, your relationships or your emotions the cause of the frightening element?
- What is the nature or quality of the threat? Is something being bitten, devoured, killed, petrified or transformed – or does something else happen? What ideas does this trigger?

- Are you familiar with the frightening thing from your real life or your personal surroundings?
- Have you ever heard of other people going through the same thing that happened in your dream? How did they survive or overcome the situation? Would this be an option for you? Why?
- From your point of view, what strategies would be useful or advantageous in facing the threat?

4. Identify the symbol or motif in your dream which stands out for you the most:

- From what personal context do you recognize this motif? What personal meaning does this motif have for you in your daily life? Can you explain this?
- Are there people you know who would interpret this motif in a completely different way – or are there circumstances under which it could mean the opposite? What feelings are evoked in you when you reflect on these differences or contrasts?
- Can you think of any proverbs that might say something about the meaning of the motif? Are you familiar with any films, books, fairy tales, myths or works of art in which this motif plays a role? What positive or negative facets might these things reveal that could contribute to the interpretation of the motif? What facets of interpretation are the most moving to you emotionally: that is, which ones have the strongest resonance for you, or perhaps even excite you?
- You can experiment with "building in" these facets of interpretation to the dream text: associate the dream motif with this interpretation. This might reveal the meaning of the dream to you.
- If your nightmare were a film, what title would you spontaneously choose for it? Would this title provide a clue to the meaning of the dream?

5. *Focus on the strongest or most striking emotion or mood you experience during the dream or upon awakening:*

Fear, panic, shock, and sometimes confusion, disappointment, disgust or shame can all play a central role in nightmares:

- What intense emotion do you or another person experience in the dream?
- Is this emotion familiar to you from your past or current life, or is it unfamiliar? In what context? Could this context have something to do with the dream?
- What happens to you when you experience this emotion in real life?
- Is there a difference between your emotional experiences in the dream world and in your waking life? What stands out for you?

6. *Look for the resources or helpful forces available in your dream:*

- Within the dream, can you recognize any resources, skills or abilities in yourself in the face of the threat? Are these resources familiar or foreign to you? In other words, do you discover any new potential of your own in the dream?
- Or conversely: are you lacking any of your usual resources or abilities; do you feel overwhelmed? What ideas does this trigger in you?
- Do you have any help or support from others? Are there any caring figures in the dream? What does this feel like? In your real life, do others sometimes come to your aid – or is this something unusual? Are you able to accept help in the dream or in reality – or is this difficult for you to do?

Acknowledgments

This book has only been possible because people gave me permission to make use of their dreams. To these individuals I offer my special thanks. In addition, I would like to sincerely thank Beate Hamburger and Anette Jörgens for their comments on the manuscript. Finally, I am grateful to my children, Jakob and Johanna, as well as my husband Michael for providing me with the time and peace without which this writing would not have been possible.

Bibliography

Barz, Helmut (1989): *Die zwei Gesichter der Wirklichkeit oder auf der Suche nach den Göttern*. Artemis, Zurich.

Böhme, Gernot (2008): *Invasive Technisierung, Technikphilosophie und Technikkritik*. Die Graue Edition, Zug.

— (2012): *Invasive Technification: Critical Essays in the Philosophy of Technology*. Bloomsbury Academic, New York.

Daniel, Renate (2011): *Nur Mut! Die Kunst, schwierige Situationen zu meistern*. Patmos, Ostfildern.

DPA (1997): "Das will ich meinem Körper nicht mehr antun". In: *Südkurier*, April 17, 1997, Sport.

Ditzen, Beate / Bodenmann, Guy / Ehlert, Ulrike / Heinrichs, Markus (2006): "Effects of social support and oxytocin on psychological and physiological stress responses during marital conflict". In: *Frontiers in Neuroendocrinology* 27, p. 134.

Dubiel, Helmut (2006): *Tief im Hirn*. Antje Kunstmann, Munich.

— (2009): *Deep Within the Brain: Living with Parkinson's Disease*. Europa editions, New York.

Egli, Hans (1985): *Das Schlangensymbol. Geschichte, Märchen, Mythos*. 2nd Edition. Walter, Olten.

Ende, Michael / Fuchshuber, Annegert (1978): *The Dream-eater*. Everyman Ltd, New York.

— (2004): *Das Traumfresserchen*. Thienemann, Stuttgart.

Fuchs, Thomas (2008): *Leib und Lebenswelt. Neue philosophischpsychiatrische Essays*. Die Graue Edition, Zug.

Franz, Marie-Louise von / Frey-Rohn, Liliane / Jaffé; Aniela (1980): *Im Umkreis des Todes*. 3. überarbeitete Auflage 2013, Daimon,

Einsiedeln. (English language edition in preparation, Daimon Verlag, Einsiedeln)

Franz, Marie-Louise von (1999): *The Cat. A Tale of Feminine Redemption*. Inner City, Toronto.

Fried, Erich (2010): *Es ist was es ist. Liebesgedichte – Angstgedichte – Zorngedichte*. 14ᵗʰ Edition. Wagenbach, Berlin.

Gernhardt, Robert (2008): *Gesammelte Gedichte*. S. Fischer, Frankfurt am Main.

Gigor, Daniela (2012): "Religionslehrer zeigte Drittklässlern Leiche. Tote Frau verursachte bei Kindern Albträume". In: *20minuten*, September 27, 2012, p. 1f.

Gribbin, John (1987): *Auf der Suche nach Schrödingers Katze. Quantenphysik und Wirklichkeit*. Piper, Munich.

— (1996): *Schrodinger's Kittens and the Search for Reality: Solving the Quantum Mysteries*. Back Bay Books, New York.

Grimbert, Philippe (2006): *Ein Geheimnis*. Suhrkamp, Frankfurt am Main.

— (2012): *Secret*. Granta Books, London.

Hillman, James *(1972/2000): Pan and the Nightmare*. Zurich/Woodstock, Spring.

— (1981): *Pan und die natürliche Angst. Über die Notwendigkeit der Alpträume für die Seele*. Schweizer Spiegel Verlag, Zurich.

Horn, Elke (2007): *Transgenerationale Weitergabe von Kriegstraumatisierungen. Wenn Trauer nicht gelingt – eine Fallstudie über drei Generationen*. Unpublished DGP-Vortrag presented on May 19, 2007.

Jung, Carl Gustav (1971ff.): *Gesammelte Werke (GW)*. 20 Volumes. Published by Lilly Jung-Merker / Elisabeth Rüf / Leonie Zander et al. Walter, Olten/Düsseldorf.

— (1971ff.): *The Collected Works of C.G. Jung, (CW)*, 20 Vols., eds. G. Adler, M. Fordham, H. Read and W. McGuire, trans R.F.C. Hull. Princeton University Press/Routledge & Kegan Paul, Princeton, New York.

Kast, Verena (1994): *Imagination As Space of Freedom: Dialogue Between the Ego and the Unconscious*. Fromm International, New York.

— (1998): *Abschied aus der Opferrolle. Das eigene Leben leben*. 2ⁿᵈ Edition. Herder, Freiburg im Breisgau.

Kast, Verena (2012): *Imagination. Zugang zu inneren Ressourcen finden.* Patmos, Osfildern.

Kehlmann, Daniel (2007): *Die Vermessung der Welt.* 45th Edition. Rowohlt, Reinbek bei Hamburg.

— (2007): *Measuring the World: A Novel.* Vintage, New York.

Kleespies, Wolfgang (2007): "Traumforschung heute: Entwicklungen und Perspektiven". In: *Analytische Psychologie.* Number 147, pp. 42–63.

Kluge, Friedrich (1975): *Etymologisches Wörterbuch.* 21st Edition. de Gruyter, Berlin.

Korczak, Dieter (Pub.) (2008): *Die Macht der Träume. Antworten aus Philosophie, Psychoanalyse, Kultursoziologie und Medizin.* Asanger, Kröning.

Kosfeld, Michael / Heinrichs, Markus / Zak, Pául J. / Fischbacher, Urs / Fehr, Ernst (2005): "Oxytocin increases trust in humans". In: *Nature 435*, pp. 673–676.

Loppow, Bernd (2003): "Ich habe einen Traum. Reinhold Messner". In: *Die Zeit,* May 28, 2003, p. 64.

Mandela, Nelson (2010): *Bekenntnisse.* Piper, Munich.

— (2011): *Conversations with Myself.* Picador, London.

Matt, Peter von (2003): "Zwischen Mythos und Medizin. Vom Schlaf und Schlafenden in der Literatur". In: *Öffentliche Verehrung der Luftgeister. Reden zur Literatur.* Hanser, Munich, pp. 187–201.

Meier, C. A. (1979): *Die Bedeutung des Traumes.* 3rd Edition. Walter, Olten.

— (1985): *Der Traum als Medizin. Antike Inkubation und moderne Psychotherapie.* Daimon, Zurich.

— (1987): *The Meaning and Significance of Dreams.* Boston, Sigo.

— (1989/2009): *Healing Dream and Ritual.* Daimon, Einsiedeln.

Mercier, Pascal (2004): *Nachtzug nach Lissabon.* Hanser, Munich.

— (2008): *Night Train to Lisbon: A Novel.* Grove Press, New York.

Otto, Walter F. (1947): *Die Götter Griechenlands. Das Bild des Göttlichen im Spiegel des griechischen Geistes.* 3rd Edition. Schulte-Bulmke, Frankfurt am Main.

— (1964): *The Homeric gods: The spiritual significance of Greek religion.* Beacon Press, Boston.

Póltawska, Wanda (1994): *Und ich fürchte meine Träume*. 2nd Edition. Maria aktuell, Abensberg.

— (2013): *And I am Afraid of My Dreams*. Hippocrene, New York.

Precht, Richard David (2007): *Wer bin ich – und wenn ja wie viele? Eine philosophische Reise*. Goldmann, Munich.

— (2011): *Who Am I?: And If So, How Many? A Philosophical Journey*. Random House, New York.

Riedel, Ingrid (2001): *Wie ein abgelehntes Kind sein Glück findet. Hans mein Igel*. Revised and redesigned edition. Kreuz, Stuttgart.

Rüther, Eckhart / Gruber-Rüther, Angelica (2008): "Psychobiologie des Traumes". In: Dieter Korczak (Pub.): *Die Macht der Träume. Antworten aus Philosophie, Psychoanalyse, Kultursoziologie und Medizin*. Asanger, Kröning, pp. 13–21.

Schmidt, Christa (2006): "Kriegserlebnisse in den Träumen von Nachkriegskindern". In: *Forum Psychoanalyse 22*, pp. 59–66.

Schredl, Michael (2008): *Traum*. Reinhardt, Munich.

Solms, Mark / Turnbull, Oliver (2004): *Das Gehirn und die innere Welt. Neurowissenschaft und Psychoanalyse*. Patmos, Düsseldorf.

— (2002): *The Brain and the Inner World: An Introduction to the Neuroscience of Subjective Experience*. Karnac Books, London.

Spies, Werner (1991): *Max Ernst. Retrospektive zum 100. Geburtstag*. Prestel, Munich.

— (2005): *Max Ernst: A Retrospective* (Metropolitan Museum of Art Publications) Yale University Press, New Haven.

Strauch, Inge / Meier, Barbara (1996): *In Search of Dreams: Results of Experimental Dream Research (S U N Y Series in Dream Studies)*. State Univ of New York Pr, New York.

— (2004): *Den Träumen auf der Spur. Zugang zur modernen Traumforschung*. 2nd Edition. Huber, Bern.

Sylvia, Claire (1997): *A Change of Heart: A Memoir*. Little, Boston.

— (1999): *Herzensfremd*. Bastei-Lübbe, Bergisch-Gladbach.

Ungerer, Tomi (1977): *Die drei Räuber*. Diogenes, Zurich.

— (2009): *The Three Robbers*. Phaidon Press Inc., New York.

Varela, Francisco J. (2002): *Sleeping, Dreaming, and Dying: An Exploration of Consciousness*. By His Holiness the Dalai Lama (Author), Francisco J. Varela Ph.D. (Editor). Wisdom Publications, Somerville.

Varela, Francisco J. (2006): *Traum, Schlaf und Tod. Der Dalai Lama im Gespräch mit westlichen Wissenschaftlern.* 5th Edition. Piper, Munich.

Vonessen, Franz (1998): *Das kleine Welttheater. Das Märchen und die Philosophie.* Die Graue Edition, Zug.

Weinreb, Friedrich (1979): *Traumleben. Überlieferte Traumdeutung.* Volumes I through IV. Thauros, Munich.

Whitmont, Edward C. / Perera Brinton, Sylvia (1992): *Dreams, A Portal to the Source.* Routledge, London.

— (1996): *Träume –eine Pforte zum Urgrund.* 2nd Edition. Burgdorf, Göttingen.

Endnotes

(The references in this book refer to the German-language edition page numbers of their sources, some of which also have English-language editions. In such cases, both editions are listed in the Bibliography.)

1   Cf. DPA: I don't want to do that to my body any more. The sudden ending of the career of a top-notch athlete who does not want to wake up bathed in sweat any longer, after dreaming of life in a wheelchair. In: *Südkurier*, April 17, 1997, Sport.
2   Cf. Póltawska (1994), p. 8.
3   Weinreb (1979), p. 15.
4   Cf. Fuchs (2008), p. 66.
5   Cf. Solms/Turnbull (2004), p. 97.
6   The so-called corpus callosum.
7   The so-called primary visual cortex, located at the back of the head.
8   Cf. Solms/Turnbull (2004), p. 98.
9   Cf. Schredl (2008), p. 83.
10 Cf. Kehlmann (2007), p.150.
11 In the case of dementia, the ego loses the ability to direct the lamp of consciousness toward specific memory reservoirs. Explicit remembering is no longer possible.
12 Cf. Kluge (1975), p. 787: The German word for dream, *"Traum"* is derived from the Germanic word *"draugma,"* meaning "illusion."
13 Cf. Meier (1985), particularly p. 63f. and p.133. The cult of Asclepius was popular from approximately the 6th century BCE until the 3rd century CE.
14 Cf. Solms/Turnbull (2004), p. 225.
15 Cf. Schredl (2008), p. 41f. The observations made by Meumann as early as 1909 were confirmed by the psychoanalyst Ernest Hartmann in 2000.
16 Cf. Kleespies (2007), p. 49.
17 Cf. Strauch/Meier (2004), p. 61f.

167

18 As long as we are awake, the EEG registers rapid frequencies, which Hans Berger called alpha and beta rhythms. During alpha activity we are relaxed; in beta activity we are alert and concentrated.

19 Cf. the results of research conducted by the team of Michael Czisch at the Max Planck Institute for Psychiatry in Munich in 2011. www.mpg.de/4613782/messung_trauminhalte (Retrieved: February 27, 2013).

20 Cf. Strauch/Meier (2004), p. 67. Strauch and Meier use the term "white dreams" when upon being awakened, a test subject in a sleep laboratory knows that he or she has had a dream but can no longer remember the content.

21 Cf. Gigor (2012), p. 1f.

22 Cf. Mandela in an interview with Richard Stengel: Mandela (2010), p. 191.

23 Cf. Strauch/Meier (2004), p. 168, 169f. and more generally, pp. 41f. and 153f.

24 And these are factors which make scientific dream research – and in turn, reproducibility and objectivity – more difficult.

25 Cf. Strauch/Meier (2004), p. 171f. The sounds were played for the test subjects three times during the REM phase at a volume below the waking threshold. Thirty seconds later, the subjects were awakened and interviewed about their dreams.

26 Cf. Schredl (2008), p. 56.

27 We are referring here to external as well as mental/emotional and physical experiences. Furthermore, it does not matter whether these experiences are conscious or unconscious.

28 Cf. Solms/Turnbull (2004), pp. 214f. and 220.

29 L-dopa is a precursor to dopamine and is metabolized into dopamine in the brain.

30 Cf. Kleespies (2007), p. 53.

31 Genesis 41

32 Heraclitus recognized this basic interplay of oppositions: everything eventually turns into its opposite. He referred to this principle as enantiodromia. Cf. Jung, GW 7, § 111.

33 And since the past and the present cannot necessarily be carried forward into the future in a linear fashion – but in fact, new and unpredictable events are also always possible – an unbiased view of past events can be very helpful when it comes to setting a course for the future.

34 Cf. Jung, GW 8, § 546.

35 Cf. ibid., 16, § 297ff.

36 Cf. ibid., 8, § 549.

37 Cf. ibid., 18/I, § 507.

38 Cf. ibid., § 469.

39 Cf. C. A. Meier (1979), p. 64, on so-called REM deprivation.

40 CF. Weinreb (1979), p. 173ff.

41 Quoted in Loppow (2003), p. 64.

42 Cf. Jung, GW 2, § 844 onwards and § 858. Jung introduced a patient in whom the complexes established in association experiments were also the subjects of her dreams. The complex revealed in the associations is the root of the dreams and of the hysterical symptoms.

43 Cf. Fischmann, in: Korczak (2008), p. 27ff.

44 *"Der Mahr"* and *"die Mähre"* are old German words for "horse." Nowadays, the German word *"Mähre"* is scarcely used; a female horse (mare) is called a *"Stute"* in German. The word survives in German in the word *"Schindmäre,"* which refers to an old, emaciated horse – the equivalent of the English "nag." There were many terms for the nightmare-bringing demon: in Switzerland, people spoke of the *"Schrat"* or *"Dockeli"*; in Austria and Bavaria, it was called *"Trud."*

45 The Sandplay Therapy Method was developed by Dora M. Kalff, a student of C. G. Jung. Sandplay therapists usually have several shelves filled with a wide variety of figures from which the client can freely select in order to construct a scene. The figures cover all areas of nature, technology, culture and fantasy. There are human figures from various cultures, with differing ages and occupations; there are monsters, houses, bridges, trees, animals and stones, to name just a few.

46 Various stories of Pan's origins exist. In most, however – for example in Homer's "Hymn to Pan" – the god Hermes is identified as his father.

47 Cf. Otto (1947), p. 105ff.

48 Cf. Solms/Turnbull (2004), p. 133 ff. The neurobiologist Joseph LeDoux describes the connections that link the object-to be feared with the fear-responses are made with extreme rapidity outside extended consciousness („First, quick an dirty pathway"). This pathway runs from the amygdalae to the periaqueductal gray – a collection of nerve cell matter in the midbrain. Once a stimulus is associated with a painful experience the FEAR system is immediately and automatically activated whenever the stimulus is encountered again, even before it is consciously recognized as such. This explains why some patients experience fear and anxiety without knowing why. LeDoux found out, that a second, slower pathway includes the cortical tissues, which allows the autobiographical self to consciously recognize what has happend and to deliberate reflexively upon it. This second pathway allows to cope constructively with fear; in other words, we a must not inevitably remain trapped in a stereotypical reaction pattern. The areas of the brain which are responsible for dealing consciously and reflectively with fear are the ventromedial and orbitofrontal regions of the frontal lobe.

49 For a few decades now, it has been possible to medically influence the fear system using so-called benodiazipines. These drugs have an anxiolytic (anti-anxiety) and relaxant effect.

50 Michael Kosfeld of the University of Zürich conducted an investment game with his test subjects, in which it was possible to win money. Subjects in whom a temporary increase in oxytocin levels had been generated through the use of a nasal spray demonstrated more trust in their game partners (cf. Kosfeld et al. [2005]). A research team led by Beate Ditzen observed that people in whom oxytocin levels were increased behaved more calmly and de-escalated conflicts (cf. Ditzen et al. [2006]).

51 Cf. Solms/Turnbull (2004), p. 145f.

52 In addition to our endogenous opioids (those naturally produced in the body), there are also exogenous opioids which we can ingest. A well-known one is opium, which is derived from the resin of the opium poppy.

53 Myths, then, are not simply fictitious or uplifting stories; rather, they contain and preserve timeless knowledge about connections within the world and within the human soul. Profound truths and laws are described in metaphorical terms. Their core messages are valid to this day; they are what C. G. Jung called "archetypes." Through myths, we can recognize structures of the soul as well as of the world – similar to the patterns in a carpet. According to the analyst James Hillman, Greek mythology, in particular, is still relevant to the people of today. The numerous gods of Olympus function as metaphors for the facets of our inner psyche. The complexity of the realm of Greek gods corresponds to our psychological situation, in which we sometimes experience ourselves as torn and contradictory in our emotions – rather as the philosopher Richard David Precht described in his book *Who Am I – And If So, How Many?* (2007). The myth of Pan is an example of the appearance of the timeless wisdom of mythology within neurobiological findings.

54 Cf. Schydlo, in Korczak (2008), p. 102f.

55 Cf. ibid., p. 94.

56 Cf. Grimbert (2006), particularly pp. 9 and 131. Grimbert's experiences are not an isolated case. For more on this subject, see Schmidt (2006) and Horn (2007).

57 Cf. Schydlo, in: Korczak, (2008), p. 97ff., a study conducted in 2007 which was probably not representative.

58 Sylvia (1999).

59 Cf. www.huna-vita.de/main/herz-geschichten.html (Retrieved: February 2, 2013).

60 Cf. Gribbin (1987), p. 198f.

61 Cf. Schredl (2008), pp. 69–72. Dr. Michael Schredl is a research director at the Sleep Laboratory of the Central Institute of Mental Health in Mannheim, Germany.

62 Cf. Jung, GW 16, § 86.

63 Cf. Fischmann, in: Korczak (2008), p. 23.

64 Cf. Jung, GW 8, §§ 474, 539 and 542.

65 Occasionally, in the process of writing a letter, we explain something important to ourselves and then realize that it is unnecessary to mail the letter. Dreams which are equivalent to such letters do not need to be interpreted.

66 Ungerer (1977).

67 Helon Habila in an interview with Ernst A. Grandits on January 23, 2013, on the program *Kulturzeit,* in connection with the *Afrikanischen Literaturtage* (African Literature Festival) in Frankfurt. www.3sat.de/webtv/?130123_habila_kuz.rm (Retrieved: January 27, 2013).

68 If the stories were banal or boring, there would be no listeners or readers for them, and the stories would quickly be forgotten.

69 Ingrid Riedel provides a detailed interpretation of this fairy tale in her book *Wie ein abgelehntes Kind sein Glück findet. Hans mein Igel* (How a Rejected Child Can Find Happiness: Hans My Hedgehog; 2001).

70 Cf. Jung, GW 16, § 322.

71 For extensive coverage of this subject, see Kast (2012). In our imagination, of course, we can pick up not only on the end of a dream but on any dream scene we wish in order to search for alternatives, escape routes or other possibilities.

72 Quoted in: Jung, GW 16, § 98.

73 Cf. Jung, GW 18/I, § 400f. One can also reenact a physical posture that made an impression in a dream in order to reveal its meaning.

74 Cf. Weinreb (1979c), p. 108.

75 Cf. ibid. (1979a), p 190f.

76 Cf. Rüther/Gruber-Rüther (2008), p. 18f.

77 Cf. Ende/Fuchshuber (2004).

78 CF. Weinreb (1979a), p. 145f.

79 Cf. Whitmont/Perera Brinton (1996), p. 72f.

80 Cf. Varela (2006), p. 129ff.

81 Even before our human parents there is nature, which prepares the foundation for our lives by allowing us to come into the world healthy, sick or disabled.

82 *Touching the Void* is a British documentary released in 2003; it appeared in German cinemas in 2004, with the title *Sturz ins Leere.*

83 Prior to his rescue, his anger motivated him to further mental reserves: he did not want to die with the song he hated, "Brown Girl in the Ring," which had been plaguing him as an earworm.

84 Cf. Fuchs (2008), p. 236.

85 "Stief-" comes from the Old High German "bistiufen" and means "to rob." The English prefix "step-" is derived from the Old English "steop-," from

a Germanic base meaning "bereaved, orphaned." Cf. Vonessen (1998), p. 129f.

86 Cf. ibid., p. 131.

87 Cf. Mercier (2004), p. 64.

88 A theory proposed by Prado, in ibid., p. 201.

89 Cf. Whitmont/Perera Brinton (1996), p. 74.

90 In newer myths, it is no longer volcanoes but the gods who endow human beings with fury. Here, too, the emotion is not a human power.

91 Fried (2010).

92 For more on the phenomenon of rage, cf. Daniel (2011), pp. 92–102.

94 For extensive coverage of the symbol of the snake, cf. Egli (1985).

95 In the case of hunger, there is anorexia, an exaggerated refusal to eat, and uninhibited eating – adiposis. As far as sleep is concerned, human beings can lose the ability to sleep sufficiently or well; however, we can also use medication to combat our natural fatigue and remain awake. Finally, sexual addiction, voluntary sexual abstinence as well as certain sexual practices show that human beings have a very different degree of freedom in terms of their sexuality than animals do.

96 Gernhardt (2008), p. 223.

97 Cf. Jung, GW 16 § 343f.

98 In the relationship between dogs and human beings, we find elements which go hand in hand with employment: adaptability, a sense of duty, loyalty and dependency. Retired or self-employed people require more cat-like characteristics – the ability to function autonomously, individuality and an active approach to the world – in order to lay claim to their own needs. Therefore, a person who enjoys serving and obeying others may have a difficult time with his or her own "cat nature."

99 Cf. Daniel 3:98f.

100 CF. Franz et al. (1980), p. 99. The latter of these was dreamed by a 54-year-old man after learning from his doctors that he only had a few weeks remaining to live. In his dream, the green forest – in full foliage and showing no signs of autumn color – was completely destroyed by a wildfire. Analogous to the dream, in his real life, the man was threatened by premature death, long before the biological autumn of his life. As the dreamer walked across the scorched site of the forest, everything was black and charred except for a red stone, which the fire had left completely untouched. There appeared to be something over which the fire could have no effect. This is one of many motifs which, according to Marie-Louise von Franz, allow us to conclude that our unconscious knows something about a life after death. Skeptics might argue that this is simply a wish expressed in a dream. Yet the sometimes brutal and merciless images which refer to the end of physical life contradict this theory of a merely wish-fulfilling character.

101 Cf. Kast (1998), p. 122.

102 A person who dreams something similar in a very different life context may ask him or herself what contradictions are at work within her – or what directions or opinions the figures might represent – and then consciously examine the alternatives.

103 Cf. Jung, GW 17, § 222.

104 Cf. Barz (1989), p. 78.

105 I also have the impression that through the presence of children, very old people sometimes experience a comforting sense of certainty that life will continue. There is a counterpart to old age which can make them happy.

106 In matriarchies, laws were enacted by Mother Earth and the maternal goddesses. They had the power to enforce obedience to their rules.

107 In contrast to the laws of nature, spiritual laws are relatively short-lived. As soon as religious convictions, societal values and the spirit of the times change, people rewrite these spiritual laws.

108 During the first two months of gestation, the gonads of the human embryo are undefined; consequently, during this early period, differentiation into either gender is possible. The Y-chromosome initiates the development of testes; if it is not present, the bipotential gonad structure differentiates to form ovaries. This only occurs near the end of the second month, when the embryo is approximately 13 to 20 cm long. The paramesonephric ducts – the so-called Müllerian ducts – remain identical for a long time until, in the course of the third month, they develop into a uterus and vagina in a female embryo; whereas, in a male individual, they atrophy and are later only recognizable as a small appendix to the male gonads. The male section of the gonadal ridge remains visible in women as the clitoris.

109 C. G. Jung identified a woman's unconscious masculine characteristics as *animus* and the unconscious feminine characteristics present in every man as *anima*. Cf. Jung, GW 9/I, § 115ff.

110 Cf. Fuchs (2008), p. 173.

111 Cf. Böhme (2008), p. 203.

112 Cf. Dubiel (2006), p. 71.

113 In Greek mythology, Poseidon is the god of the ocean and the initiator of earthquakes. He represents violent, deep-seated emotional outbursts.

114 Cf. Matt (2003), pp. 187–201. If, on the other hand, we lie in bed unable to sleep, we are forced to think or brood constantly.

115 Cf. Dubiel (2006), pp. 94 and 129.

116 In mythology, the chimera is a hybrid creature consisting of both human and animal elements.

117 When a man wanted to get rid of a transplanted hand which had been attached to his body in a complex operation because he was unable to

experience it as a part of himself or integrate it into his life, some people chastised him as being thankless or called him unreasonable.

118 Modern technology allows us to penetrate previously invisible realms and thereby reveal things which could not be seen in the past. At the same time, we are creating new invisible worlds by bundling radiation or manufacturing new substances which can be dangerous to human beings and nature.

119 Quoted in Spies (1991), p. 9.

Aniela Jaffé

Death Dreams and Ghosts

200 pages, ISBN 978-3-85630-580-2

A collection of death dreams and ghost stories were gathered and presented to C.G. Jung and the author, who approaches this fascinating material from the depths of her analytic experience.

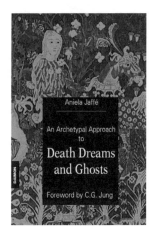

"... among the Swiss, who are commonly regarded as stolid, unimaginative, rationalistic and materialistic, there are just as many ghost stories and suchlike as, say, in England or Ireland. Indeed, as I know from my own experience ... magic as practiced in the Middle Ages ... has by no means died out, but still flourishes today ...
I can recommend it to all those who know how to value things that break through the monotony of daily life with salutary effects, (sometimes!) shaking our certitudes and lending wings to the imagination."
– from the Foreword by C.G. Jung

We are left in the overpowering presence of a great mystery.

Tess Castleman

Sacred Dream Circles

A Guide to Facilitating Jungian Dream Groups

This is a handbook about participating in group dream modalities. Practical exercises included in each chapter anchor the step-by-step instructions given for running a safe, yet deep and meaningful group process with or without a professional facilitator. Care is taken to discuss shadow projection, clear communication, and confidentiality issues. Topics include: nightmares, recurring dreams, childhood dreams, and synchronicity. Creating the tribal dream, where participants interweave their dream material in a complex yet boundary-safe fabric is the quintessential goal of this companion volume to the author's previous book, *Threads, Knots, Tapestries*.

224 pages, ISBN 978-3-85630-731-8

Harry Wilmer
How Dreams Help

"Growing numbers of people are fascinated by the dream world. From psychological scholars and analysts to spontaneous groups and cults, the dream has a compelling voice. ... I make the point in this book that our dreams are our most creative inner source of wisdom and hope. ... The criterion for selection is simply that each one illustrates a common human life experience that all readers have had or are likely to have."
— from the Introduction by the Author
192 pages, ISBN 978-3-85630-582-6

C.A. Meier
Healing Dream and Ritual
Ancient Incubation and Modern Psychotherapy

C. A. Meier investigates the ancient Greek understanding of dreams and dreaming, Antique incubation and concomitant rituals.
In this greatly expanded version of his classic work, Ancient Incubation and Modern Psychotherapy, Meier compares Asklepian divine medicine with our own contemporary psychotherapeutic approaches to dreaming. He elucidates how the healing cure was found in the very core of illness itself — a fact of invaluable significance today in both medicine and psychology.
In helping us to recognize the suprapersonal aspects of illness, the dream is shown to reveal a transcendental path to healing.
168 pages, 10 illustrations, indexes, ISBN 978-3-85630-727-1

Healing Dream and Ritual is one of the most significant and lasting witnesses of how far beyond immediate psychology the implications of Jung's work stretches. This book is, in my feeling, as important for today's healers as was the early work of Paracelsus to the redirection of medicine in the Renaissance.
— Sir Laurens van der Post